BEATING
JOB

How to turn
your work into
your passion

BURNOUT

PAUL STEVENS

BEATING
JOB

How to turn
your work into
your passion

BURNOUT

PAUL STEVENS

Printed on recyclable paper

VGM Career Horizons
a division of *NTC Publishing Group*
Lincolnwood, Illinois USA

This book is for those who are searching for
new and liberating horizons and
are prepared to take considered risks.

Library of Congress Cataloging-in-Publication Data

Stevens, Paul. 1941–
    Beating job burnout: how to turn your work into your passion/
Paul Stevens.
        p.   cm.
    Includes bibliographical references.
    ISBN 0-8442-4474-0
    1. Job satisfaction.   2. Job stress.   3. Career changes.
I. Title.
HF5549.5.J63S73 1995
650.14—dc20   95-801
                                                                CIP

Published by VGM Career Horizons, a division of NTC Publishing Group
4255 West Touhy Avenue
Lincolnwood (Chicago), Illinois 60646-1975, U.S.A.
©1995 by NTC Publishing Group. All rights reserved.
No part of this book may be reproduced, stored in a retrieval system,
or transmitted in any form or by any means,
electronic, mechanical, photocopying, recording or otherwise,
without the prior permission of NTC Publishing Group.
Manufactured in the United States of America.

5 6 7 8 9 0 VP 9 8 7 6 5 4 3 2 1

About the Author

After twenty-one years' employment experience as a personnel manager dealing with the problems of employer/employee relationships in the UK, Canada, and Australia, Paul Stevens created the Centre for Worklife Counselling in 1980. His concern for individuals and their search for satisfaction in work motivates his daily counselling and teaching activities and his writing. He has become nationally known as a counsellor, broadcaster, and author of 27 publications on worklife and career management issues. While continuing his counselling practice, he has been hired by organizations to advise on their career development activities and to assist in organizational restructuring where it has an impact upon the job satisfaction of employees. His national Worklife Agency Network now provides a range of career development services to individuals and employers in all states of Australia. Paul continues to extend his work to include career support to members of religious orders and consultancy services to Australian state governments, devising innovative measures which assist both employer and employee to cope with change.

An Explanation—Worklife

The organization I founded in 1979, the Centre for Worklife Counselling, often provokes comment about its name. The term "Worklife" was chosen to reflect our continuing work in research, counselling, training, and publishing material which relates to improving people's enjoyment of their employment activities and other aspects of their lives. We do not accept the traditional view of career counselling—that is, to help people acquire satisfaction only from their working hours. We believe that occupational satisfaction can only occur when a person's total needs are included in the assessment of what is lacking and what needs to be done to increase inner well-being, improved relationships with others, and effective performance both at work and non-work activities. The word "life" in Worklife means our focus is on the total person. The word "work" relates to the roles in which the person is involved (employee, student, homemaker, and citizen) and his or her environments (workplace, educational institution, home, community). Ours is a holistic approach—we try to consider all features of a person at the same time as maintaining a respect for personal privacy by the use of nonthreatening inquiries into thoughts and circumstances.

Contents

PREFACE

There are a growing number of books being published on worklife strategies that offer some simple and readily comprehensible instructions. Such books can be entertaining and insightful. Unfortunately, few of these books have a sound empirical basis for their analyses of people's career behaviors. This book is based on a different approach.

Beating Job Burnout explores the career transition journey that a typical person undertakes when resolving difficulties with his or her worklife. To assist this journey, I will share the approaches I have learned through experience, in a practical, rather than a scientific, manner. These approaches have involved considerable design, experimentation, and evaluation activities.

During the past 15 years I have counselled over 2,000 people on a one-to-one relationship basis, and more than 2,800 people have participated in Career and Life Planning Workshops that I have conducted. In addition, many hundreds more have completed career analysis questionnaires I have designed, and their responses have been analyzed and interpreted. Regular talk-back radio programs have allowed me to learn more from others about their worklife difficulties and career transitions. Each person who has shared his or her problems and triumphs has enabled me to be the conduit by which many more may benefit.

What I do is help people to manage change in their lives; to alleviate the pressures, to guide people so that they can find out what they really want to do and how they can go about making that happen. In doing this, it has become clear that people who learn how to love their work make a significant contribution to others, while growing into selfhood. As you will read, clients of my counselling practice have played an integral part in what unfolds in this book. They contributed the quotations I have placed in the book as beacons in the career transition journey. My clients overcame both internal and external obstacles to become happier in their worklife by cultivating self-respect and inner security and developing a commitment to their talents and their self-worth.

This book has been developed from the experiences of my clients. I make no claim that what follows are the only or best methods of resolving worklife difficulties or curing all the symptoms of stress that cause "burnout." But I do have the conviction, through observing the effect on the lives of many other people, that the material in this book, when acted upon, will enhance the reader's life and improve his or her well-being.

Thank you to those who have allowed me to be a companion during their career transition. You have contributed to an enthralling journey, from an office in a converted bedroom in my home to my situation today. My helping work now extends not only across Australia and New Zealand but several times each year to the United States and the Nordic countries, particularly Sweden.

Assisting others to resolve worklife difficulties has increased my enthusiasm and respect for those I feel privileged to help. It is a most satisfying way of earning a living. It has been fulfilling to be a pathfinder, with contributions from those I have helped, amongst the complexities of adult career transitions. Again, many thanks . . . and there is so much more I have yet to learn and share with others. While writing this book about you and other people, where and how you work, I have, of course, been describing my own odyssey.

Paul Stevens
Mosman, Sydney

PART *I*

WORKLIFE EVENTS AND CAREER HAZARDS

· ·

- A day of work
- The meaning of work
- Career journeys
- Expected events
- Unexpected events
- Non-events
- Life stages
- Pressures from others
- Dual-career couples
- Career burnout
- Job content
- Employment environment
- Lifestyle contradictions
- Career renewal
- Career development theory
- The career transition experience
- Bibliography and useful further reading

· ·

. . . .

When we consciously choose to do work that we enjoy not only can we get things done, we can get them done well and be intrinsically rewarded for our effort. Money and security cease to be our only payments.

Marsha Sinetar
Do What You Love, The Money Will Follow
(Dell/Bantam, 1989)

Identifying a satisfying career is not the outcome of gimmickry but of careful self-examination not only of capabilities and knowledge but of values and priorities. A satisfying career is invented, not found and exploited. It is pre-tested and pre-examined for its potential to provide opportunity for personal growth.

Sidney A. Fine, The W. E. Upjohn Institute
for Employment Growth Research, USA

We live in a world of organizations. In less than a century they have come to dominate our lives. Community and Church have been replaced by the work organization as second only to the family as the most important influence on our lives.

Professor John W. Hunt
London Business School
University of London

. . . .

A Day of Work

It is Wednesday morning, close to 8:30 a.m. In a few minutes, in my counselling room, I will be greeting a new client, Sandra. She has been referred to me by her doctor. It will be the beginning of another journey that will involve me in the life of another person. Later in the morning, Ted is due to return for his third consultation and report on progress with the homework I gave him. He phoned earlier in the week to say how emotionally exhausted he felt, yet he was sure that logic and clarity over the future direction of his career were emerging.

Joseph is due at midday. He was fired three weeks ago by the employer with whom he had worked for fifteen years. Well, not actually fired in a strict legal sense: together with ten other colleagues, he was made redundant on a Friday afternoon and was required to leave his employer's premises the same day. Economic conditions within his employer's industry, not his work performance, had led to his dismissal. His wife, having noticed a rapid lowering in his morale, phoned last week to seek advice on how to encourage her husband to visit me. "He is so proud that to seek such help will be viewed as weakness," she said. This is a common plea and there were a number of tactics that I was able to recommend. They worked, and Joseph made an appointment.

After seeing Joseph, there'll be a break from counselling while I visit an employer in the early afternoon to discuss the findings from an extensive survey of the staff of one particular manager. They were asked about their attitudes towards their working life and their firm. The findings are strong in tone and potentially very useful, that is if the manager views the data as a basis for changing certain entrenched procedures in order to improve morale among his work force, a move that will benefit both employees and employer. He might, on the other hand, take the results too personally and become annoyed with his staff. It should be an interesting session.

The day will conclude with Elizabeth. She has established a pattern of meeting with me every six months after work to discuss her current situation, her successes and failures and the current threats to her well-being at work. She will come well prepared, with an agenda or concerns, and, following our previous consultations, with alternative plans of action for each of the concerns which will be used as a basis for our discussion.

A speech to final-year students and their parents is scheduled for 7:00 p.m. at a local school. If the evening follows the usual pattern, I will find myself responding to questions about the parents' personal concerns about their own worklife as much as their children's.

The paperwork on my desk won't receive much attention today. I am aware of the urgency conveyed in the letter from a woman living on an outback property who has abruptly found herself in a situation where she must relocate to a large town or city and seek employment. She wants advice on how to achieve this. There are also fifty foolscap pages of writing from Bill, a forty-eight-year-old schoolteacher who was referred to me after he had hit a child in his classroom and was subsequently suspended from teaching. Bill's guilt and loss of self-esteem overshadow his attempt to work out why he hit the child and what else he can do. I read five "life" stories each week as part of my commitment to clients to interpret or audit their worklife experiences and life management concerns.

All of today's clients are on a journey, each at a different point along the path to finding a resolution of career-related matters which are causing varying kinds and degrees of stress and burnout. The effect of these problems is not restricted to the individuals. Their loved ones, and in some cases their employers, are anxious for positive solutions to their particular career dilemmas.

It's a typical day ahead of a worklife counsellor and consultant to organizations on career development support systems. The job title I've created for this type of work is the Sadness to Joy Facilitator! It's not in the government-compiled *Dictionary of Occupational Titles* but, if required to describe it, my explanation would be along the following lines: helping people with worklife problems by means of a rational step-by-step approach. As the person takes a journey of self-exploration, I assist in evaluating his or her options and implementing choices. This approach is not only an intellectual one. It incorporates the emotional, cognitive, and psychological processes that involve the total person and the environment in which he or she lives. Structures for thinking and remembering are provided in a way that prevents the person from dwelling unnecessarily on negative experiences.

The Meaning of Work

So many times I have heard comments such as: "It isn't possible to have a job you really love." "You work because you have to not because you want to." "It is expecting too much out of life to have an occupation you love." Each time, I feel sad—sad that the person has this viewpoint, that so much of their working lives must be a burden to them, that they are being beaten by burnout. Work for them is not a personal growth experience. I do acknowledge, however, that it is hard to achieve a more positive viewpoint when faced with a difficult economic environment and when the people you are close to believe that work is just a way of earning money—a way of earning the maximum amount of money, given one's qualifications and skills, to provide sufficient income and flexibility to lead one's chosen lifestyle.

Work is basic to our sense of social and personal identity. After a long and considered contemplation of the human condition, Sigmund Freud nominated work and love as the two essential ingredients of a happy and well-adjusted personality. Just as satisfaction in love requires work, so, in turn, we can argue that work satisfaction requires love of what we do in order for us to feel complete.

Expectations of work satisfaction have changed. A survey undertaken by Eena Job among those over eighty years of age in a suburban area included a review of their expectations when they were working. Ms. Job is the author of *Eighty Plus: Outgrowing the Myths of Old Age* (University of Queensland Press). If she had undertaken the survey among a lower-age group, the following quotation would probably be quite different and reflect the change in what we expect from our worklife. "The concept of work satisfaction was foreign to respondents in the survey. Many took pride in doing a fair day's work for a fair day's pay, and if they stayed with one firm or organization over a long period, they developed a sort of loyalty to its interests. But the work itself was seldom questioned for its value either to the individual or to society. They seemed to regard a paycheck, or the opportunity to earn one, as less of a right than a matter of good fortune. Work, as they saw it, was simply a necessity."

Today, most of us who are engaged in work want much more. Yet, to arrive at a point where the unique characteristics of a person are comfortably matched with a particular occupation is a complex aspect of one's journey through life.

As we change in physical abilities, personal circumstances, and maturity, so do our wants, needs, and preferences change. Our work environment is also far from static. The supply and demand for certain sets of skills and experiences fluctuates. Occupations disappear and new ones emerge as economics and technology influence the manner in which work is carried out. Our economy affects the prosperity or otherwise of different industries and in turn the requirements of employers for trained people.

What is known is that in order to attain emotional satisfaction from work, people need to become competent in influencing the direction of their worklives: to become less reliant on their employers to provide work satisfaction and to make efforts themselves to determine what it is they want. Most need assistance with this process, and they are likely to require such assistance several times during their lifetime. Those in the profession of career guidance and worklife counselling provide services to meet this need.

The attitudes regarding work expectations that prevail in our society are at odds with what I have learned about the joy of finding fulfilling work. Once a person has found work satisfaction, there is little room for the views that one should not work too hard or too much; that enjoyable times in living are reserved for weekends or vacations; that work is thankless drudgery; that it is from the boss that you find out how you are doing; or that one is one person at work and a different person outside work. I find my work a joy. I believe that others can do so, too, with the right amount of personal effort. Persistence, stubbornness, and gritty determination are crucial elements of this effort. I believe that our economy can benefit from people finding this joy and, as a result, working enthusiastically and more productively.

Work for me is a creative experience, a deeply valuable pursuit. It has hardships, setbacks, and irritations, but these are less of a bother to me. My energy levels are consistently high. I amaze myself by the amount of work I accomplish. I am working at what I really enjoy. Time with my family and trips to the countryside are scheduled into my week, not set aside to a specific period in each year. Work is an activity which allows me to use the more truthful parts of myself . . . the real self. The present concerns me more than the future. Work is a fulfilling expression of who I really am. The pressures, time demands, and fluctuating financial circumstances are part of this joy. None is pleasurable in isolation, but as part of the whole scheme of things each is an integral part of this experience.

Work provides me with a synergy of the skills I prefer using; many of the skills I have, and used well in the past, I no longer use, nor do I want to. I am being selfish in what I do and in turn feel selfless in the benefits of my work to others. I am well aware of my weaknesses, but do not dwell on them. I work with my strengths. I am not ever angry about my work; rather it is the avenue I use to express my developing personality. I express my positive emotions through what I do. I am determined to do what I choose to do even though easier financial rewards beckon from other directions. Yes, I am addicted to my worklife. I do not crave status or approval from others. When it occurs, I enjoy the feeling but do not consciously seek it. I am not conceited about finding work I really like doing. I paid a price to reach this state. I earned the right to be joyful in what I do.

The following description of a person totally satisfied with their worklife was written so eloquently by Marsha Sinetar in *Do What You Love, The Money Will Follow* (Dell/Bantam, 1989). I know I have not yet reached this pinnacle, but I do know I am well on the way, while assisting people on the same journey.

> The traits found in common in the vocationally integrated, actualizing personality are:
>
> - The individual possesses a firm sense of identity, can "stand alone," be alone; he is fully present in the moment and his work.
>
> - The individual is able to and willing to consciously choose to do his work, and this very ability to make conscious choices, to take the consequences for the choice, is precisely the mark of his maturity, his inward strength, his independent, whole personality and at the same time is one of the elements which activates his future growth.
>
> - His choices are a prerequisite to his feeling that he has power, that he can "create," that he has options, that he can make a difference, that his actions—however slight—matter, if only in his eyes. Again, it is from these attitudes and from his values that the individual gains the strength to contribute stability and something from within himself to the world.
>
> - At his best, the individual is truly himself, more completely authentic and integrated as a personality, and thus is able to bring the complex of his full, entire self (i.e., all his energies, talents, courage, attention, sub-selves, etc.) to the work at hand. As a result he has more to give through his working efforts than the

one who withholds attention, talents or loyalty or who is working "just to earn a living," or merely to make ends meet. He has more to give because he has a completely integrated self to give.

- Work becomes a devotion, a labor of love, and indeed—whatever the person himself might call it—a spiritual exercise because the individual's concentrative powers, his choices, actions and values, are motivated, prompted and fueled by love, and his service, as it were, is simply the enactment of this positive life-force. His being or essential self lives in all he does.

· · · · · · · · · ·

I have often felt that I am bursting with potential but have no catalyst to realize it. Like an arrow waiting to be fired. It would, therefore, appear that I have to become the bowman as well.

· · · · · · · · · ·

Career Journeys

I need money to live
I need stimulation from achieving
I want to learn about people, the world, myself
I want to explore my potential
I want to be challenged intellectually, spiritually, emotionally
I want an activity that is all mine
I haven't enough money to explore all of the above without working for pay from an employer

Each day that I am not consulting with organizations or fulfilling lecture tour commitments, I participate in the career journeys of individuals attending my counselling practice. Such days are very precious to me. First of all, the individual facing me has shown me respect by thinking that I may be able to assist. Second, I learn from all of my clients, whatever their ages, circumstances, or personalities, and whatever stages they are currently grappling with in their career transition journeys. I learn about them but I also learn about their employment environments. There would be many managers and heads of departments who would envy my access to information about the attitudes of their employees and the effects of their managerial styles. Thank goodness there are no "insider trading" aspects to worklife counselling!

People who come to consult me have taken a brave step. It is often easier to drift passively along in an unsatisfactory situation at work and hope things will turn out for the best, than take action. But inactivity is not a recipe for worklife satisfaction. A far more fruitful endeavor is for an individual to take control of his or her own career progress, develop a distinctive style, and learn how to influence others so that they can a behave in a way which is more satisfactory to his or her needs. A career is not built on what appears to be attractive in the world of employment but on what is good within the person. This book is about sharing information on how this can be achieved.

Our career journey commences before we leave secondary education and make the transition from school to higher education or employment. It involves a complex interplay of sociological and psychological aspects. These include factors such as family social background, hometown, sex role stereotyping, self-esteem, ethnicity, ability, the perceived influence of parents, teachers, and peers, plus self-assessment of our scholastic competencies. This multifarious analysis is undertaken either consciously or unconsciously at a stage in life when we lack sufficient maturity to analyze these factors for ourselves in a logical, systematic manner.

The career path choice is made, or made for us, often in an environment which makes it seem as though it is irrevocable. Our destiny for the next forty years is ordained, or so it appears to us at the time.

Some will make a commitment to this career path choice in a reasonably rational and purposive manner. Others will drift into a career, or decide seemingly spontaneously. All will start the journey with little or no awareness that it is but one of many significant worklife decisions we will make before we come to the end of our career journey. Throughout this journey we will make many career transitions, some self-initiated, others as a reaction to events in our lives.

Expected Events

The major life events we usually expect to be part of adult life are marrying, becoming a parent, starting a first job, retiring, and dying. Statistics are regularly gathered and published by government agencies about these expected events, such as age of marriage and dying.

As we traverse childhood and youth and reach adulthood, each of us develops an expected timetable for these events. Because of a host of variables, our life may not in fact conform to this expectation. Depending on these variables and our attitudes, we adjust, either comfortably or not, to expected events which do not occur on our personal timetable. When we commence work for the first time and begin to learn about life at work, we similarly form a vision of where our careers may take us and calculate approximately when we will reach certain stages in this career. The unpredictability of living means that we will encounter many unexpected events, even non-events, which will have a great bearing on our worklife.

Unexpected Events

A concoction of disillusionment, frustration, dissatisfaction, breakdown in marriage, tumultuous living and the desire to try a larger and more prospect-filled locality prompted me to migrate and alter the pattern of my career.

Secondary schooling, in my personal experience, focused on preparing me for expected events in my adulthood. Previous students were frequently quoted by my teachers as role models because of their successes, but the intimacy of their journey to these successes was not shared. The quest for high scholastic achievement was advocated as the key to future achievements. I do not recollect one lesson which encouraged discussion about recovering from disappointments in life's journey. The legacy of this education was one of striving at all times to do one's best and the inference that good results, that were also good for me, would follow.

My naïveté did not last long once I had started full-time employment. The memory of my early career setbacks is clear, and even thirty years later I am still a little resentful that I was so ill prepared to accommodate them. It is a similar story for many other people, as I know from listening to my clients and reading their biographical writings. In fact, I find it very useful to help them remind themselves of how many setbacks they have experienced and conquered. I use the worksheet "Career Setbacks" (Figure 1) for this purpose. It doesn't encompass all the career setbacks that can be experienced, but it goes a long way to helping clients appreciate the distance they have so far travelled in these terms.

You may like to pause in your reading and complete this worksheet for yourself.

The degree of career satisfaction we experience is determined by several factors. When we accept a position with an employer or set ourselves up in self-employment we are prepared to provide our time and talents in return for remuneration and an expectation of good feelings and success. In this arrangement there is an expectation of a fair trade. One gives of one's self in an expectation of receiving. In reality, our perception of how equitable the trade is changes over time. It changes because of unexpected events of a desirable and/or undesirable nature: speedy promotion, lack of promotion; surprise pay increase, marginal pay increase; new skills and learning of an enjoyable nature, no significant change in knowledge level; etc. We continuously try to manage these situations. Every now and then the experience is not comfortable. The unexpected event has changed the nature of the trade in a way that we regard as unsatisfactory, debilitating, or causing discomforting stress. We arrive at a state of job burnout. When this occurs we have the choice to persevere without initiating any change or take action to redress the balance of the trade. Many do not see this situation as an opportunity for choice but depend on their employer to implement the remedy. This is an abdication of personal responsibility and an erroneous view; employers never state explicitly in their employment offer that they will provide happiness or stress-free job tasks.

Employees with contracts or years of experience have planned on comfortable retirements funded by their employer—and now they are looking for work.

Whatever career dilemma we are experiencing today needs to be seen as part of the tapestry of life, not as an isolated unexpected event.

Career Setbacks

Action: Circle, underline, or highlight all you have experienced.

poor performance appraisal . . . job application rejection . . . made short list but not job offer . . . work colleague told tales . . . flirtation at office became widely known . . . experienced anxiety attacks at work . . . lost out on training course selection . . . insomnia . . . did not confirm boss's expectations . . . lost enthusiasm for Mondays . . . inadequate salary review . . . ignored office politics and suffered . . . sexually harassed . . . failed probationary period . . . learned about attractive transfer opportunity too late . . . made redundant . . . observed taking home office stationery supplies . . . damaged company car . . . fell out with general manager's secretary . . . read negative notes about myself on boss's desk . . . did not make sales quota . . . acted silly at company-organized function . . . selection interviewer talked too much about self . . . a bad reference . . . career burnout . . . career boredom . . . career path blockage . . . experienced reverse discrimination . . . report returned marked "unsatisfactory" . . . fell asleep at a meeting . . . exceeded budget . . . salary decreased . . . employment agent disclosed my job search . . . dead-end job . . . regarded as "over-qualified" . . . own business failure . . . overheard denigrating my boss . . . employer promises unfulfilled . . . misinformed about reality of job . . . victim of office politics . . . fired! . . . spotted falsifying expenses . . . lost a good boss . . . lost addresses of business contacts . . . concluded chose wrong career . . . became "chained" to my job title . . . company relocation caused extended commuting . . . current employer heard I was looking around . . . reluctant to delegate . . . didn't get on with own job, but meddled in others' . . . argued with managers . . . changes in company policy reduced career opportunities

Action: Recall how you recovered. Would you act differently now? How?

Figure 1. Career Setbacks Worksheet.

We can bear up more readily under the strain if we see the dissatisfaction and confusion we are currently experiencing over worklife, or the hurt we feel over a recent negative situation at work, as only one thread in the overall fabric of our lives.

The value of unexpected events in our lives is immense. They continually influence our character and how we relate to others and our environments. That is not to say that we should put off or even avoid career planning, but that we should harness what we have already experienced and learn how to manage setbacks more effectively. And, of course, all the unexpected events we have experienced are not necessarily of a negative nature or outcome. I write with some fervor that what I first perceived as a negative unexpected event brought on by job burnout—being fired from my employment as a personnel director 16 years ago—has subsequently led to an enthralling and deeply satisfying new way of earning and living.

When most people accept an employment offer they rarely anticipate that it will lead to mobility from this employer to another. In the past decade in non-recessionary times, U.S. government statistics show that 25 percent of those working had changed employers a year later. Almost half of the people in jobs had been in them for less than three years. The significance of the data raises considerable questions as to what causes employees to resign and seek out alternative employment. What unexpected events occur for so many when they are still in the early stages of a position with a new employer?

I believe that this degree of restlessness derives from low levels of satisfaction in their worklives. It also points to the general inability of people to work out what actually constitutes job satisfaction for themselves, so that they are more thorough in their choice of occupation and employer.

Crises brought about by unexpected events and change occur all through life. We are continually at the beginning of, in the midst of, or resolving transitions caused by them. Some are initiated by us due to changed circumstances, some by the actions of others, including employers.

In worklife, when an unexpected event occurs, it is very easy to sink rapidly into depression. Many of us behave as if we have no control over life events or our reactions to them. We seem to expect negative events to happen and do not believe we are able to prevent their recurrence; we see ourselves as having no control over how or why they occur. But control can be regained. By taking a structured approach to analyzing what has gone wrong and what needs to happen to change the situation, vitality for work can be restored. Involuntary loss of employment precipitated for me the most unhappy period of my life.

My struggle with shame and unhealthy self-pity, loss of self-esteem and an inability to cope with rejection did later evolve into a determined search for methods to help others either prevent such occurrences or recover from them. I recollect most vividly my feelings of anger about the way I felt.

I felt I didn't deserve such an abyss of unhappiness. My feelings of defenselessness appalled me, but I seemed unable to change them. I retreated from loved ones, friends, acquaintances, although I needed the help of others to restore me after this unexpected event in my career. I have seen and consoled many others experiencing similar unwelcome emotions. I have loaned my companionship and skill to assist their recovery. I now know that the therapy required is a structure for our thinking, support, and action. It has felt like a mission to explore, design, and evaluate such structures.

Non-events

Most people grow from teenage to adulthood expecting to marry. Current national census figures reveal that nearly 30 percent of the total adult population have never married. This has prompted book publishers such as Collins to publish in 1989 *Why Aren't You Married?* by Jillian McFarlane. Among the many reasons given in reply is the theory that many people are not marrying because of their pursuit of personal autonomy. The expectation of being married changes along the way and prompted one of my clients to comment: "I have very much two things running side by side: this ability to be independent and successful and not worry about parenthood, and a conditioning from my childhood. These have been continually fighting each other."

The life events that occur "on time" according to our expectations do not usually precipitate a crisis or self-questioning about their appropriateness. It is the unanticipated or non-events that cause problems. For some, the incongruities between expected, unexpected or non-events represent new freedoms for their worklife actions, but for others the results are new uncertainties, debilitating stress, and confusion as to appropriate courses of personal action.

I have not accumulated sufficient money to retire to a tropical island, or climbed Mount Kilimanjaro in Kenya, or taken a year off to wander unhurriedly through other cultures or pursue at leisure my interest in Renaissance literature. Nor have I fathered three children. I am sure you can recite a similar litany of plans, fantasies, dreams, and intentions which have not eventuated. What is important is how each of us accommodates their non-occurrence. If we dwell too much on what might have been it will reduce our energies and commitment towards the realization of what is yet to come. It will hinder our likelihood of working out what it is precisely that we want to happen and then working hard to increase its likely occurrence. This implies taking stock of how far we have journeyed, auditing who we are today, and determining what really matters to us. Along this life journey we have changed, adjusted, compromised, set new goals a thousand times. What has been lacking for many of us is a reliable structure, or method, by which we might undertake this task and so move on to reducing the incidence of non-events, turning them into expected events in the process.

That wise man of Stratford-on-Avon, Shakespeare, expressed this so ably in the sixteenth century:

· · · · · · · · · ·

There is a history in all men's lives,
Figuring the nature of the times deceased;
The which observed, a man may prophesy,
With a near aim, of the main chance of things,
As yet not come to life; which in their seeds,
And weak beginnings, lie intreasured.

· · · · · · · · · ·

Life Stages

Many researchers have endeavored to classify as expected events the crises or career direction problems we are likely to face as we travel the journey through life, and to link these events to age. Hence it is expected that we will seek adventure more than meaningful work in our early twenties, have a "mid-life" crisis between the ages of 35 and 44, feel a form of silent despair in our early fifties, a fear of becoming irrelevant in marriage and work, and in our sixties experience trauma through the loss of work in our lives. Life stages are depicted as an orderly succession of expected events in many textbooks as if they will happen on cue for all of us. Not only does this mislead, but it can cause some to abdicate all responsibility for setting out to change things, and to account for their particular feelings with the explanation that life is like that and one has to put up with it, or that better things are ahead.

My experiences in counselling and the access I have had to the details of many hundreds of lives have taught me that there is no distinct age period at which these psychological issues occur. One can experience at 24 the trauma usually associated with mid-life crisis (35 to 44), or feelings of irrelevancy at any age, and so forth. The timing, I have learned, depends more on life events than chronological age. Age, I have found, is an unreliable indicator of what people will feel at various points in the journey. The subjective nature of aging means that some will perceive themselves as much younger or much older than their actual age. This is caused by a myriad of factors such as mental and physical health states, personal circumstances, the value placed on employment activities, and whether or not we are striving to satisfy the expectations of others rather than the uniqueness of our individual selves. The scenarios and altered perspectives which occur in our lives are so varied and variable it is not possible to anticipate them according to any reliable timetable.

· · · · · · · · · ·

At 33 I am too old to be a whiz kid with promise, yet I lack the runs on the board to be considered a nascent high flyer.

· · · · · · · · · ·

In anticipating certain events, some people may feel they haven't "made it" if not promoted to chief executive officer or company president by age 35, while others may delay parenthood in order to consolidate their career future, and feel anguished about this decision. A consciousness of our age still prevails, but in the context of personal career management we have the choice for it to be either a stimulus or a brake upon our worklife activities.

At any age, our feelings reflect our personality. Living in a rapidly changing society such as ours requires flexibility in adjusting to both external social realities and the discernible changes within us.

How we react at different ages to unanticipated and non-events differs from one person to another. The timing of events in our adult years is so variable that we cannot assume that particular transitions will occur at specific ages, or that one person's behavior will be consistent with that of another's when experiencing a similar transition. Throughout adulthood, age is a poor indicator of the likely timing of events, a person's interests, needs or work status. The nature of a career transition, whether recovering from lost employment, losing out on a coveted promotion, or reacting to the change of ownership of an employer, is more dependent on how it will alter our role, relationships, routines, and assumptions. We cope with the transition according to our reaction to these factors and the resources we have at the time, such as money, self-confidence, emotional stability, personal philosophy, values, and self-perception.

Change brings about a reaction within us and the good or not so good effects of this reaction will differ over time. Job loss, unsatisfactory relocation, and other career setbacks require that when helping people recover, their resources and weaknesses need to be examined in relation to their particular situation, their sense of self, their support relationships and the way they perceive particular strategies. In each of these four areas lies the opportunity to diagnose which aspects need more attention than others. By systematically sizing up each of them we can learn how to build on our strengths and reduce the negative effects. Every change or career setback is an opportunity for personal growth. But many have difficulty in perceiving this and often need help to restore their morale and take the steps that will accelerate their recovery.

Our changing society has brought about changes in the social meanings of age and age-appropriate behaviors. Consequently, career renewal can be initiated at any age. You're never too young to burn out at work—and it's never too late to beat it. Whether implementing a job change or career realignment, age has more to do with the assumed attitudes of current or prospective employers than with the individual. Traditionally, there has been a tendency to segregate people into age groups, and activities such as education, parenthood, work, and retirement are seen as relating to particular age groups. These attitudes ignore the real-life situations of people. The 1989 Nobel Prize winner for Literature, Camilo José Cela, endorses this reality when commenting: "Man has as many lives as years he's lived, and today I am in my seventy-third life." Just as more people are marrying, divorcing, remarrying through their sixties and seventies, so can occupational activity be altered with realizable opportunities for new worklife experience. There should be more media exposure of such career behaviors to accompany the portrayals of the Veterans' Olympics and sexagenarian first-time authors. Even in their sixties, singers such as Tony Bennett and Buddy Greco are redefining career life cycles by continuing to be successful.

This blurring of traditional life periods has not met with a corresponding change in pace of employment regulations relating to age. The difficulties faced by those pursuing career renewal in the latter period of life are more exacerbated than eased by employment law and employers' personnel practices. Yet progress is being made. In America, legislation forbids employers to retire compulsorily an employee before age seventy. In Australia where I live, two states have enacted legislation, the Older Worker Act, which forbids employers to retire compulsorily an employee at any age other than for proven health reasons or non-performance of job tasks.

Pressures from Others

Many of us are living other people's lives. In some cases the dominant influence is from some family member already deceased. In carrying out career analysis as a prelude to career planning, it is important for you to identify to what degree you have absorbed the expectations of others. The quest is who you really are today, what you really want and expect from yourself. As none of us is devoid of memories, childhood experiences, family membership, or current relationships, we need to identify who has influenced us and continues to influence our values and self-concept, and by how much. We need to think about the significant people in our life and what they expect of us in terms of our worklife. What do others want us to be, to do, or to think? Once this analysis has been completed it is easier to determine what is our own thinking and what is inherited or absorbed from others, and thus needs to be identified as such.

Let the words of some of my clients over past years convey the danger of entrapment in working to please others:

. . . .

I don't feel comfortable with the idea of personal success and opportunities. I have never been encouraged to aim high but to feel protective of others and to see material wealth as a bit immoral and unfair.

I need to overcome the conditioning of my upbringing . . . the belief that as a wife and mother my needs are less important than the needs of those in my care . . . and to think or act otherwise is being extremely selfish and should make me feel guilty.

Because I did not choose to follow my father into his business he took no interest in my career choice. Emotionally, he withdrew his support.

At the time I felt it was expected of me to replace my lost priestly vocation and the choices that I saw as being acceptable to others were to study medicine, law, or accountancy.

Success and well-being are not the family norms; struggle and subservience are. Succeed only a little; too much success is dangerous, so the individual must withdraw . . . the norm becomes inaction, procrastination, and confusion.

What I am trying to articulate is the appalling realization that I have been brought up to believe that if you do a job well, you will be satisfied.

All my life I have hidden behind a wall. It hides what I see as my deficiencies from other people; I have always been quite sure that I had an awful lot of deficiencies to hide. I could never let people see what I was really like. They would never love me or like me on my own merits; I felt that the only way I could be loved would be by pleasing people all the time.

So this wall hid my true feelings from others. I was never allowed to display strong feelings; someone might not like it. I just had to put up with things I didn't like, because then things in the future would be so much nicer in comparison. So, if I got angry, I'd think I was at fault, feel guilty, and hide behind my wall again. One of the buttresses of this wall was "being a doctor." A doctor is supposed to hide her feelings in order to function properly; at least that was how I saw it.

So I think that for most of my career I've coasted along, not really enjoying medicine, not ever doing what I wanted to do, whatever that was, protected from the dangers by my wall, waiting for my white knight on his white charger to come and take me away. That way, I wouldn't have to displease my father by telling him I didn't like medicine. I would cope with sticky situations by ducking out, rather than meeting them head-on.

But, it didn't quite work out like that. I met a man and took the first "risks" of my life when I left my secure government job, sold my house, got married, and moved to .... But we lasted only a short time. So there was I, alone in a strange town, no income, no job, no house, no friends. What hurt me really badly and still does was that my parents didn't give me the support that I needed—they expected me to comfort them.

I began to realize then that the way I had lived my life, trying to please other people, doesn't work. Pleasing others at your own expense doesn't make you happy. You'll only be happy when you live to please yourself. That does sound selfish, but I think you must be selfish at least to a certain extent to survive as an individual.

All this happened three years ago. It was then that I decided to start pleasing myself. I obtained work in landscape gardening and enrolled part-time in related studies.

. . . .

Significant Other

It is not unlikely for a person grappling with a worklife problem to try to disguise their situation from the significant other person in their life. A deteriorating career or work-based relationship, even loss of a job, may be covered up by the maintenance of a daily routine. Not only does this usually lead to surprise and conflict at some stage when the true situation is discovered, but such persons have also denied themselves the opportunity to verify their self-understanding with one who knows them well. Whether residing together or dating regularly, the significant other in a person's life has to accommodate the changes a person may make when resolving dissatisfaction with their worklife. The significant other is likely to be more supportive if allowed to contribute to the career transition activities and the decision making that will be required at several points along the way. Conversely, some are in relationships where the significant other is affecting their worklife negatively. No empathy is shown for the burden carried by the person in attempting to resolve their worklife problems.

. . . .

Although I have thought a great deal about my career, I seem to come to an abrupt halt when the personal aspects come into it. I feel that I have drawn the short straw in relation to my husband's career interests.

. . . .

Dual-career Couples

My research reveals that in many dual-career couple situations it is important to the male that his partner develop her occupational life just as he follows his own career pursuits. This is not the case in every partnership. A relationship is often threatened when the female accelerates her career progress or becomes more successful then her partner. In these days when having a child is a matter of choice and when career participation for both can be more enthralling and demanding than ever before, those who pursue dual-career arrangements need to debate and review goals and plan regularly in order to achieve and resolve a host of conflicting demands.

To keep a desire for worklife fulfillment in a closet, to surrender or subjugate career-related personal growth denies both members of a dual-career partnership a special enrichment from the relationship. It denies respect for each other as unique individuals.

Dual-career couples are unlikely to be free of tensions arising from worklife, but even these can contain excitement as well as difficulty, their resolution providing a feeling of shared accomplishment, innovation, and creativity as well as relief. Vicarious gratification can be derived from the partner's achievements while striving for and achieving one's own. Dual careers do offer each person two sources of career satisfaction. But they require a special effort to communicate and resolve any conflicting demands that threaten their success. For those in dual-career partnerships who put a premium on worklife achievement, training in career development and planning is important. Anticipating career blockages and coping with or avoiding career setbacks, self-preservation skills and office politics are subjects worth studying. The greatest threat to mutual satisfaction in dual-career couple situations remains the fact that the concept of domestic backup continues to be primarily the burden of women. We are still far from an equitable situation in the sharing of household chores.

New patterns of living and changes in employment environments have brought about a new set of problems for those living alone or in partnership arrangements. The trend towards more egalitarian, sharing kinds of partner relationships is demanding complex career management strategies to ensure that both parties fulfil their particular worklife ambitions. The cost of career-related individuality should not necessarily be an increase in either our divorce rate or partners separating.

Women are reaching senior management ranks at the same time that increased pressures at that level are affecting them and men alike.

Complete the following worksheet "Employment Environment Pressures" (Figure 2). Check the pressures you are currently experiencing.

The drive for increased productivity and economic recovery means long hours at work are now the norm. Time for self, one's partner, and non-work activities is growing less.

Employment Environment Pressures

Action: Is this representative of your situation at work?

	Yes	No
• Executives so busy that they don't have time to support the managers who report to them	☐	☐
• Leaner organizations following downsizing, resulting in reduced opportunities for advancement	☐	☐
• Greater competition between peers, reducing inter-personal cooperation and imperiling teamwork	☐	☐
• Frequency of restructuring, causing morale reduction as rumors proliferate	☐	☐
• Cutbacks in resources, leading to situations where more is expected to be accomplished with less	☐	☐
• Time—and approval—for professional development activities is a reducing commodity	☐	☐

Figure 2. Employment Environment Pressures Worksheet.

Setting clear goals among dual-career couples means you are both setting out to exercise more control over the direction of your lives, improving your abilities to foresee the future, increasing tolerance for new situations, and extending the capacity for both to become the selves you truly are.

The impact of clear goals on dual-career couples is significant. Health, happiness, and income are strong reasons for striving for a career and for working hard to clarify why each is doing so. Clear goals also are useful in developing cooperative and constructive relationships between the individuals. The clearer the goals, the stronger the motivation to make a relationship work. Energy is more productively focused.

If you are in a dual-career partnership, assess your relationship by completing the following worksheet, "Dual-career Partnership Assessment" (Figure 3).

Dual-career Partnership Assessment

Action: Check yes or no for each item as you consider your relationship.

	Yes	No
• Partners see their partnership characteristics as a balance that is mutually enhancing	☐	☐
• Neither sees the other as being in the service of the partner	☐	☐
• An understanding is worked out about what sort of balance of achievement is tolerable	☐	☐
• It is personally important to one that the other develop a satisfactory occupational life (i.e., an emotional investment)	☐	☐
• In situations of conflicting demands, the advantages/disadvantages are considered for the family as a whole	☐	☐
• A strategy is evolved that allows for each partner's development while both strive for an equitable balance of strains and gains	☐	☐
• The arrival of the first child is well coped with as a pivotal point in the dual-career commitment	☐	☐

Figure 3. Dual-career Partnership Assessment Worksheet.

Career Burnout

The range of career-related problems that people experience and have to solve for themselves is becoming formidable in both number and complexity. Not surprisingly, many of us hanker for former times when we simply went to work and got on with the problems arriving through the in-trays or via the production process. Now, it's as if we need the learning gained from a psychology degree, plus a sympathetic therapist, in order to survive a week on a payroll!

People experiencing negative career stress are disinclined to meet deadlines at work, to increase their output, or to strive for improved effectiveness at their job tasks. The danger takes many forms. They may not even be conscious of their behavior and may be unable to interpret the signs from others that their continued employment is in jeopardy. Information is withheld from them and conflict can result.

Yet an inner awareness tells us that life at work cannot be easy. Work satisfaction des not happen automatically. There are strategies for career enhancement which are also appropriate for preventive action or recovery from setbacks. Time spent reviewing them is worthwhile and makes people less prone to adverse events in the employment situation. Overcoming the phenomenon of worklife burnout is one of them.

Career Stress

Burnout is characterized by emotional exhaustion, coupled with cynicism, and occurs among individuals who spend a lot of time under conditions of tension and negative stress. It is more likely to occur when we invest too much of ourselves in the job. Burnout diminishes our feelings of being worthwhile.

The popular myth is that it only occurs among those in the helping professions such as nursing, medicine, teaching, and social work. In fact, it can affect anybody who feels the necessity to maintain a veneer of interest which covers the opposite set of emotions; in other words, a pretense or behavior which does not reflect how he or she really feels about recurring situations at work. Add that to a declining interest in the work content, sometimes simply because it has been completely mastered, and burnout can occur. The cause can be either in the job content or the employment environment or a combination of both.

Characteristic Symptoms

Career burnout is not simply the drained feeling you have at the end of a busy day—it's a progressive cycle of energy depletion and loss of vitality, affecting the emotions, body, and spirit.

A person who is in a state of continual fatigue—the sort of fatigue neither nine hours' sleep nor a week's holiday relieves—could be a victim of burnout. It is often accompanied by feelings of extreme frustration. A dedication to work which is not being met by internal rewards of self-esteem, or a perceived lack of external indicators from others that efforts are appreciated characterize a state of mind now diagnosed as burnout. The person is probably trying harder and harder but accomplishing less and less.

The emotional self may be depressed, easily disappointed, or consistently irritable. There may be reduced personal responsibility for outcomes, work alienation, and lack of personal accomplishment. Physical symptoms may include fatigue and sleeplessness, or symptoms that will surprise and concern the sufferer, who will probably want to deny that the exist.

The relentless pursuit of one goal without the balance of other objectives in life will eventually force a burnout victim to take "time out" to analyze his or her condition. If not, a friend, relative, or work associate is likely to intervene and attempt to make the person realize that there is a problem. Such assistance should not be rejected. It could trigger a chain of events which help the person to avoid collapse from physical exhaustion or mental stress, or prevent him or her from turning to alcohol or drugs or actions which risk employment status. Burnout becomes a real career hazard when sufferers realize that, emotionally, they have nothing left to give. Until this point is reached, the symptoms may have been obvious to others but not necessarily to the victim.

Other symptoms of burnout are emotional withdrawal, particularly from the significant other person in life or from an employers' customers or clients. Less patience with family members and friends, talk of the "great escape" to a different way of living (a small farm in the country often features here), or a realization that the pretense of outward appearances is costing a lot in emotional energy are other signs.

· · · · · · · · · ·

An increasing reluctance to go to work was coupled with apathy as I did not feel my usual inclination to strive to change or improve work situations, for myself or others.

· · · · · · · · · ·

Burnout Recovery

- Learn and adopt tension-dumping routines from a stress expert

- Develop a plan for change

- Set an objective for behavioral change and implement it

- Evaluate outcomes of these new actions

- Review career AND life management activities, personal values, and direction

---

Figure 4. Burnout Recovery Checklist

Returning to Real Self

Early actions should include getting regular exercise, eating better, obtaining more sleep and energy-restoring rest. Finding some time alone is just as important. The length of time is not so important, but the privacy and opportunity for reflection within a state of calm are.

Those who resolve to sort things out can spend a lot of time trying to do so, only to find their thoughts circling a fixed issue like moths around a lamp, with the most important aspects eluding them. In this situation we need a structure for our thoughts, a systematic method for ordering them, and the discipline of writing them down. The role of those engaged in human care counselling is to be a companion, skilled in helping throughout this journey of self-discovery.

As a coping method, burnout sufferers should be advised to vary routine at work as much as possible within the confines of the job and to start guarding emotional energy. They should take more frequent breaks from demanding tasks and talk about their feelings with someone who's not going through the same problems. They should not suffer in silence. A treat is a good idea, a pleasurable event, excursion, or purchase they may have been thinking about for some time. Such treats can only be a temporary or short-term solution, but they can do wonders to restore the flagging spirit.

. . . .

I was in an office-based job before my last position and it was one deadline after another. When you finished one set, the next set was overdue—you never got ahead. The list of TO DO was always longer than the list of COMPLETED.

. . . .

An unrelenting feeling that the job demands behavior which the inner self is really not wanting to provide is conducive to burnout. Perhaps the initial challenge has wilted considerably since taking on the current job.

Without obtaining new knowledge and skills of a nature and content which we would choose, rather than feel we have to obtain, humans are very susceptible to feeling low. A sustained period without an increase in learning or new challenges leads to forms of depression. At the chronic stage, the burnout phenomenon is at its most personally dangerous unless action is taken to alter this psychological pain, particularly if sufferers are trying to prevent others they interact with at work from noticing their dilemma. Here is a short questionnaire (Figure 5) entitled "Analyze Your Current Job," which will help you to audit whether or not you should take some corrective action.

Job Content

Our quest is to pinpoint the real sources of our dissatisfaction. Once identified, it is easier to focus on bringing about change. We need to distinguish whether it is our occupation, i.e., the job content, or the employment environment where we carry it out which needs to be changed.

Our level of satisfaction with the job content of our career can be seen as a series of stages in which our interests, needs, motivations, behavior, and attitudes change over time. It is useful to assess at what stage we are when reviewing whether a change in what we are doing is appropriate or not. Here are explanations of the four stages.

Analyze Your Current Job

	Yes	No	Unsure
• Can you see clearly when you have done a good job?	☐	☐	☐
• Does the work give you a sense of achievement?	☐	☐	☐
• Is it obvious to you if the job is not done to standards acceptable to your boss?	☐	☐	☐
• Are you dependent on co-workers to do this job well?	☐	☐	☐
• Does the job require planning tasks more than one week ahead?	☐	☐	☐
• Is the job a stepping stone along your desired career path?	☐	☐	☐
• Is the job preparing you for more responsibility of the nature that you want?	☐	☐	☐
• Is it easy for others to see you do your best work in this job?	☐	☐	☐
• Is it realistic to expect to earn more money within the next six months?	☐	☐	☐
• Is your desired career move from this job likely within the timeframe you have in mind?	☐	☐	☐
• Is the job:			
a. requiring you to use the skills you prefer using?	☐	☐	☐
b. important to the organization?	☐	☐	☐
c. giving you responsibility for a complete piece of work?	☐	☐	☐

Action: More than three answers of NO and/or UNSURE indicates action on your part is necessary to reduce the likelihood of career burnout.

Figure 5. Analyze Your Current Job Questionnaire.

Exploration Stage

This involves making job preference choices, settling down into a routine, growing in familiarity with the tasks of the occupation, and making conclusions about whether it appeals as a long-term prospect. Some choose a career with care, others react to circumstances and "find" themselves within a particular career path. In this stage your enthusiasm grows in acquiring professional knowledge in your job; you apply a high degree of energy to the development of skills.

Advancement Stage

Here you actively cultivate internal and external contacts and resources to help perform the job better and improve your eligibility for advancement. This usually involves promotion and an increase in the difficulty of work tasks undertaken. It is also likely you will have to deal with rivalry from co-workers seeking similar goals. Conflicts between career and non-work time allocation begin to materialize. There is usually a desire to seek changes at work that are considered important. The refinement of one's skills is pursued eagerly. Feedback from others is strenuously sought.

Maintenance Stage

This can be a complex and confusing period as you reorganize your thinking in relation to your choice of occupation. You may be conscious of and apprehensive about perceived competition from colleagues and subordinates for similar jobs or even your own position. Ambitions require adjustment and this process can be characterized by loneliness, even when close support relationships exist. Eagerness to implement change becomes less urgent to you. You consider the dangers of failure and loss of respect from colleagues before acting on or withdrawing proposals for changes in work methods. The main clue to identifying whether the maintenance stage has been reached is when the new skills and knowledge you gain in your job are no longer as stimulating as they once were and no longer retain your interest to the same degree.

Decline Stage

We move into this stage if the career action steps required at the maintenance stage are not clear or are ignored. Many realign their career directions and so avoid this stage. Others, aware of considerable inner discord, persevere in familiar job surroundings but are concerned that their waning enthusiasm for this kind of work will be spotted by those who have "power" over their fate. Some people are able to get through this stage comfortably by making the effort to consolidate their careers, not by seeking higher risk positions, but by shifting from a power role to one of consultation and guidance to others. Their interest changes to wanting to influence others through a lateral relationship rather than one of a command nature. Others identify, negotiate, and implement changes to the content of their job (i.e., job enrichment). Without such adjustments, people are in the danger zone of, for example, declining self-esteem, waning performance of job tasks, and the risk of being fired or retrenched. At its worst, psychosomatic symptoms occur such as sleeplessness, increased irritability, sometimes an increased intake of alcohol, pills, or tobacco.

We may find ourselves in the early stages of our occupation (i.e., job content), and no change is required to improve the contribution of our job content to our well-being. The problem may lie in where we carry out the job content.

Employment Environment

We need to evaluate regularly the culture or "atmosphere" of a workplace in relation to our feelings. Is it one with which we are becoming compatible or should change be initiated? Employment cultures which demand constant perfection and output at the same high level day after day without some variation are the source of many burnout victims.

The recessionary times that are being experienced in most countries are causing the human side of many, but not all, employment environments to be grim. Employees within them are often frustrated, disillusioned, and increasingly despondent. A discontented present seems coupled with an uncertain future. Each person in this situation needs to decide whether he or she is going to tolerate this or set out in a careful search for alternatives more conducive to how that individual really wants to feel and where he or she really wants to work.

A downsized organization is only as good as the enthusiasm of employees remaining to manage and produce.

Concerns about our level of satisfaction in our worklife can prompt us to consider a change in career. There are many ways to beat burnout—don't rush out and quit your job. This may not be the appropriate action. The source of our dissatisfaction may be our choice of employment environment—not our occupation. Consequently, it is important to assess the current stage of the relationship we have with our employer before deciding our next career action step. Here are explanations of the four stages of our relationship with an employer.

Exploration Stage

This stage is the process of learning what really matters at your place of work, the nature of interpersonal relationships with work colleagues, the boss's boss, and learning what is expected—and how it is rewarded or criticized—in the performance of the job tasks. The atmosphere or "culture" of the work unit and the organization is keenly observed and assessed by you. In this stage you form a vision of the likely future with the employer and define your career, professional, and personal goals within this organization.

Advancement Stage

Here you are likely to feel accepted by the organization. More challenging assignments are allocated, responsibilities increase. Contacts with other staff—some in senior management positions—are easier to develop. The "informal power" nature of the organization becomes clear and you assess whether you like it. There are several indications given to you that you are valued by the organization. Promotions may occur reasonably easily. You feel compatible with the nature, apparent values, and practices of your employer.

Maintenance Stage

This stage is characterized by having achieved a series of accomplishments in the organization's employ and in relations with senior staff. You feel able to predict accurately how the employer will act in most situations regarding staff and different economic circumstances. Some aspects of your worklife may be stressful. Some disappointments in your relationship with your employer may be experienced. You may begin to feel less sure of predicting how the employer will react to internal events affecting operations and your career progress.

Decline Stage

Here you may produce work which is no more than minimally expected. Your cynicism about the employment environment may be quite pronounced. You are likely to experience a range of emotions and on occasions be inconsistent in your behavior. Helplessness in influencing positive change may be experienced. Less enthusiasm or non-participation in social functions connected with your employer may occur. A feeling of detachment from the organizational goals and culture may occur. Low commitment to your employer may characterize how you feel about working there. You could be realizing that your values, skills, and abilities are not a good fit with the organization. It is no longer worthwhile to devote extra effort to achieving your employer's objectives. On occasions, your name may be left off distribution lists or invitations to meetings and/or functions.

Lifestyle Contradictions

Career dilemmas are a subset of the total lifestyle needs that people have. These needs differ from one person to another. Lifestyle needs are complex and relate to such matters as how we prefer to use time, who we prefer to relate to and be with, how we react to a specific geographical location for home and worklife. They form the basis for mapping out who one is and comparing this with what one does. For many the conflicts between their lifestyle needs and either their job content or employment environment, or both, become a burden. When this occurs and the incompatibility is distinct, negative stress effects result.

Economic hard times prompt employers to demand more. Many employees are questioning their lifestyles where they are having to respond to this demand and not getting back any apparent gain. The price of stress does not seem to be balanced by a fair trade in terms of material wealth. Even job security, but no job satisfaction, is not enough for many when their lifestyle needs are not being met.

· · · · · · · · · ·

To overcome the worklife hardships I felt, I withdrew into a very private and vivid inner world nurtured through reading, films, radio, and nature itself. Flora, fauna, sea, sky, and terrain.   · · · · · · · · · ·

Career Renewal

We should not allow a state of worklife dissatisfaction to continue, pretending to ourselves that it is not a problem. An excerpt from Joseph Conrad's *Lord Jim* is particularly relevant here:

> No man engaged in a work he does not like can long preserve many saving illusions about himself. The distaste, the absence of glamour, extend from the occupation to the personality. It is only when our appointed activities seem by accident to obey the particular earnestness of our temperament that we can taste the comfort of complete self-deception.

Increased self-awareness is the way to a satisfactory solution; those who don't know themselves well will bend back and forth under the pressure at work. A process of analysis which uses our past and present to map out a plan for the future is needed, not a casual reflection on how far we have come or what success has brought us.

Such a plan should contain much more than work goals and schedules for their accomplishment. It also demands that people identify and rectify what is missing in their non-work activities. Lifestyle management is the key to recovery or, more positively, protection from burnout. People need to develop a well-balanced schedule of daily experiences which includes more of what they enjoy and less of what they dislike.

Such self-analysis may well identify a previously buried desire for a different way of earning a living. It may challenge assumptions about our physical and mental capabilities. The person with a strong sense of self is more likely to cope with stress. Sense of self comes from increasing our knowledge about self. This also contributes to raising our self-tolerance and the level of confidence we project to others. Positive self-awareness does not remove the anxieties associated with our life but does provide a strength for tolerating them and better managing the stress they cause. So, embark on a journey of self-discovery and clarify your values. Visit your local bookshop and select a range of self-help books to guide you in this process and transition to increased inner wisdom. Several titles I and my clients have found useful are listed in the bibliography at the conclusion of Part 1. This can be a bulwark against the "outside" world. Reflect on the last time you took time out and paused to consider how far you have come and where you are heading in all aspects of your life.

Recall what you really enjoyed learning at an earlier stage of life. Consider enrolling as a student in a new course or hobby, for the sake of your own interests rather than its value to your career. Get going on a planned program of reading in your favorite subject. It doesn't matter whether it is the lives of Egyptian pharaohs, Renaissance philosophy, or growing ground-covering plants. The contents' appeal to the individual is the important consideration in choosing the topic.

Variation is the key to burnout recovery. The quest should be to include in life more of what you prefer, rather than what you feel obliged to do. Don't simply blame others, the situation, or "them" for the state of your depleted emotions. Taking personal responsibility for career management and lifestyle is the route to more satisfactory and fulfilling living. A reevaluation of career direction and implementing a thoroughly considered option can bring about improvement in both psychological and physical disorders. The reports from my clients following their career transition journey have convinced me there is a direct connection.

Those who choose to ignore burnout symptoms risk more than hurting themselves. But by pacing themselves, introducing diversions, planning and implementing change, and communicating with others, they can go a long way towards avoiding damage to relationships they really care about.

· · · · · · · · · ·

I have been forced, not unwillingly though, to formalize a semiconscious awareness of myself. Consequently, I have acknowledged certain personal characteristics as important to change. I am now taking a much more imaginative approach to my next career action incorporating them.

· · · · · · · · · ·

It is unlikely that any single activity will keep me happy in the long term. About three years is the maximum before I feel the need for a change.

· · · · · · · · · ·

Career Development Theory

There is as yet no single comprehensive theory, or model, that explains all the factors of how a person—teenager or adult—can be reliably "matched" to a specific career or make a career change that is guaranteed to be successful. Career development theory is a young science. The findings to date are more in the nature of collected observations and regularities, which are not always consistent with each other.

Career development is therefore a multi-theory science; no single theory has an absolute majority of agreement among researchers and career counselling practitioners. Despite this disparity of views, career development theories do have the useful function of helping us to organize empirical observations of how people's careers are chosen and develop.

Two quite divergent approaches in career development theory have been developing for some time. The one with the longest history may be termed the matching of people with the content of jobs. The gen-

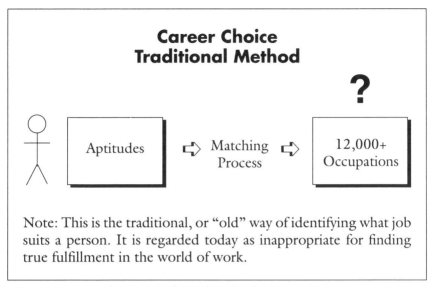

Figure 6. Career Choice—Traditional Method.

eral focus of this procedure is to determine the skill aptitude and temperament requirements of particular occupations and match these with the characteristics of the individual. Figure 6 illustrates this.

The development of psychometric testing originates from this approach and provides standardized measures to assist this assessment process. It assumes that individual differences in ability and personality can be systematically related to the variations in occupational categories. It assumes also that workers in different occupations will have different psychological attributes and their adjustment to work is maximized where attributes and job demands are matched accurately. In the past decade, however, the use of measures of intelligence, aptitude, and temperament in career guidance has declined and a number of studies have challenged the notion that pyschometric test data can adequately predict occupational success, satisfaction, and work performance.

The main premise used by those researchers and counsellors who favor the trait and factor job matching approach is that there exists one ideal job for each person and that people's interests and abilities do not change over time. These two factors are, the theorists maintain, most responsible for career choice and satisfaction. If special talents, levels of ability, and intelligence are measured, the process is merely a matching with an occupation which fits.

The opposing career guidance approach places much more emphasis on counselling as a skill and on the self-search effort required of the individual and less on the "interpret, tell, and sell" practices of the other. It demands skill in enabling the person to solve his or her own problems rather than providing the answers.

The objective is to enable people to make worklife decisions for themselves. The key difference is the view that vocational choice, adjustment, and coping is seen as a lifelong process. Self-concepts change, preferences alter, and the initial career choice is unlikely to be sustained throughout a working lifetime. Individuals may wish to initiate a change of occupation and/or the nature of their employment environments; or, through necessity, they may need to learn and apply career change techniques more than once. The main emphasis is on helping people to learn how to assemble necessary data about themselves, make career decisions, establish effective work relationships and, when appropriate, be successful at attaining promotion, transfer, or an alternative employer. The underlying theme is that career choice and decision making are not concerned with a single life event but with a continual process of personal change and learning.

Career development literature over the past decade has contributed to the growth of understanding of career issues within the overall fabric of a person's life, and incorporates the social and cultural context in which the person lives. There are several researchers, academics, and career development practitioners who have contributed to the current level of knowledge about career choice among adults.

I have attempted to illustrate the more well-known writers and the titles of their methods in the following chart (Figure 7) "Modern Career Choice Methods." Also included are several other less well-known career development theories generally referred to as sociological and economic theories.

The career theories based on what can be termed a lifespan perspective maintain that career choice and subsequent career progress is a social process. The nature of one's schooling, family socioeconomic background, the influence of family members and close friends, and the expectations a person evolves from them are seen as the prime determinants of occupational choice, one's level of attainment, and what prompts a person to make a career change or career path realignment.

Modern Career Choice Methods

Trait and Factor
- General Trait and Factor (Darley & Patterson)
- John Holland's Typology
- Myers-Briggs Typology
- Work Adjustment Theory (L.H. Lofquist & R.V. Dawis)

Lifespan
- Donald Super's Stages of Adult Development
- L.S. Gottfredson's Theory of Career Development

Career Decision Making
- Social Learning Theory (J.D. Krumboltz)
- Individualistic Perspective (D. Tiedeman & A. Miller-Tiedeman)
- Sequential Elimination Theory (I. Gati)

Psychodynamic Theory (M.L. Savickas)

Personality Development Theory (A. Roe)

Sociological and Economic Theories
- Accident Theory (several authors)
- Status Attainment Theory (several authors)
- Human Capital Theory (several authors)
- Dual Economy Theory (several authors)

Adapted from *Applying Career Development Theory to Counseling* by Richard S. Sharf (Brooks/Cole Publishing Company, 1992)

Figure 7. Modern Career Choice Methods.

My work in worklife counselling tends to favor the multi-career, lifespan, and sociological approach. Yet the career transitions my clients take do not conform to the pattern of one particular career development theory. My observation is that career actions are more likely to be prompted by unexpected events or non-events in a person's life. In fact, as many as 70 percent of my clients initiate career review and subsequent actions leading to some form of career content change as a result of a negative setback in their worklife or in personal circumstances outside their employment environment. A minority initiate career review as a self-help measure and plan their career horizons when their worklife is relatively satisfactory. In many instances people need strong incentives to make major life and career decisions. Some will walk around a swimming pool, initially reluctant to jump in and experience a few moments of cold before enjoying a swim, but will take the plunge; others will have to be pushed. Where I do find agreement with the career development theorists is that the concept of a career being continually "upwardly mobile," in other words, of a linear nature leading to more responsibility with each career action, is not true for the majority of people at work.

Consequently, I define a career as a sequence of work experiences, paid and unpaid, which:

- requires an activist approach
- incorporates your task preferences
- has elements of well-researched risk taking
- includes self-set goals and schedules
- obtains feedback from others
- necessitates self-evaluated performance
- provides psychological success
- combines characteristics external to you with changing factors within you
- should be a continuous adventure

A more succinct way of defining a career is as a sequence of work experiences in which one identifies a changing array of personally attractive satisfiers beyond simply earning a living.

Many believe they have no career. Having a career does not mean anything significant to them. "I have a job," they say. They have jobs that earn a living but contribute little more to their inner well-being and satisfaction with their journey through life. Something is missing, something elusive. Hence their admission, "Others have careers, I have a job." They acknowledge other people can have a career, but they cannot. Many people have many careers but lack resolution on one particular career in which they can not only be competent but feel they are contributing more than just a trade of skills for pay. They are not prepared to close off some possibilities for the sake of realizing others. Closing off possibilities is a prerequisite in order to create an effective design for our life management. Others are in never-ending preparation for a career. "My reward, feeling better about what I do, will come one day if I simply work harder and let luck play a part."

A person who has a career has made a declaration, first to self and then to others, about a particular direction in their worklife—a set of purposes. They do not dream of a career—they have brought reality into their dream. It takes hard work, emotional investment and determination to work out a direction. It takes courage to search deeply into self and then make a choice from the options everyone of us actually has—whatever our education, socioeconomic circumstances, and personal constraints may be.

The transition journey brings many rewards. One of the most important is that we come to realize that we do, in fact, all have a career. In identifying a career we declare an identity that we intend to create for ourselves. This identity that we formulate will benefit us and those around us for whom we care. Our career is our personal description of ourselves, regardless of the label—our job title—imposed on us by our employer or a dictionary of occupations. Declaring what career we have is a purposeful statement that helps us give meaning to our lives. Once declared, we also know that we will need to review it again and again and, if necessary, realign or change our career declaration.

In observing hundreds of people grappling with their career dilemmas and progress towards choosing between a number of career action options, I have noticed that both external and internal considerations influence their decisions, such as:

External (visible to others)
- Occupational title
- Employment benefits
- Status
- Ability
- Behavioral style
- Pay
- Location
- Influence over others
- Career direction
- Lifestyle

Internal (private to the person)

- Self-concept
- Goals
- Motivation
- Preferences
- Frustration
- Unexpected events
- Relationships

- Hopes
- Values
- Transferable skills
- Feelings
- Expected events
- Non-events
- Perceived expectations of others

These external and internal aspects are interdependent and undergo continual change. Personal career management involves the success with which we manage the interrelation of these different factors. Critical to this is the need for an adequate knowledge of self. Everything we need to know to resolve feelings of dissatisfaction already exists within us. The challenge is to identify reliable methods of taking stock of each of the aspects of our internal self and relate them in a systematic way to the external characteristics. Hence, we ourselves, more than employers, create and maintain attitudes which lead to a deeper sense of annoyance, sometimes bitterness, and feelings of being trapped in a particular career situation, unless we undertake this essential self-exploration as part of the career transition journey.

There are several beliefs which influence the methods which I use in assisting others with this self-exploration. In summary they are:

- It is important for people to plan their futures.

- A life plan should retain flexibility. For example, it is likely that the students leaving secondary education this year will change careers an average of 5.2 times during their working lifetime. Those currently in their forties are part of a generation making an average of 2.8 distinct changes from one occupation to another during their employment life.

- People need to develop the ability to overcome career-related setbacks; they should not hesitate to seek out guidance facilities when they experience job loss, confusion over career direction, or insufficient knowledge. Pride can inhibit a person seeking such help, as they may have been taught that they should solve such dilemmas themselves.

- All will perceive some form of constraint to their career progress. These constraints are likely to include one or more of the following: poor health, wrong socioeconomic origin, inadequate or inappropriate education, gender stereotyping, wrong age, excessive commitments to non-work circumstances, poor self-concept, geographical location restrictions.

- Learning the skills of career transition and career management is an integral part of total personal development.

- Self-knowledge is critical for successful decision making.

- If people are to derive satisfaction from their work they must have a sense of accomplishment. Among other things, this implies that they need to be familiar with valid self-assessment and goal-setting techniques. Without a clearly defined target, there will be no sense of accomplishment when it is reached. In fact, the individual will not know he or she has reached it.

- Though the match between occupation and person may be accurate, the employment environment in which the job is carried out may not be suitable. Many will experience negative job elements such as: feelings of being in a rut, undervalued, or overstretched; apparently closed doors to advancement; uncongenial supervision and/or co-workers.

- Though the match with occupation and the employment environment may both be accurate, an inability to incorporate the needs and interests that they have outside the work situation may inhibit satisfaction with their career choice.

- People need to have and, in the face of constant change, maintain an accurate knowledge of occupations that will suit their unique qualities.

There is no longer one job, one career, for all our adult years. For career security and to achieve inner well-being, we must strive to be more independent and take care of our own careers. In essence, we have to give security to ourselves, not wait in futile anxiety for others to deliver it. Self-empowerment is the recipe for healthy living and working for at least the next decade. Through a regular assessment of our job content, employment environment, and lifestyle needs, and by taking appropriate action as indicated, we nurture and bolster our self-esteem and are better able to live and work with others.

The Career Transition Experience

I view work as an extension of myself. I need a career to recognize my own self-worth.

A career transition is any career step which alters your current worklife activity or pattern. You may willingly initiate it or it may be thrust upon you by events outside your control. Consequently, the time period for a career transition varies widely. Some take a matter of weeks, others typically take one to two years to resolve. A career transition produces feelings of disorientation, alters the perception of self and demands changes in previously established career direction assumptions and behaviors.

It is a period of reconstruction which affects our self-view, the way in which we establish our personal identity. It is a disruption to our normal working pattern and involves some redefinition of who we are and how we are going to work. One's personal values, self-worth, and feelings of security are brought forward and require an audit. This audit may prompt us to alter the direction of our career and make significant changes in our work and life management. This redefinition will provoke some degree of anxiety even when the change may be actively sought.

Change, even when it's for the better, is rarely easy. But if we don't change we could be resigning ourselves to living with our dreams unrealized, which as well as leading to a sense of dissatisfaction can also result in depression and low self-esteem. Changing what is unsuitable releases the log jam that hinders us from achieving our goals. Most unsuitable things can and should be eliminated, though it may seem less painful, less risky, in the short term to stay as we are. Our attachment to those things that give us a sense of security can be the most formidable of the log jams to be removed.

A career transition affects more than ourselves. Our loved ones are rarely unaffected by our emotional state and the way in which we resolve to take career actions. Bonds with professional associates and work colleagues are also likely to be affected.

Career transitions feature forms of grieving for the security that we are leaving, then a healing time, which is followed by a renewal of spirit and enthusiasm. A change within us of some sort is unavoidable, be it large or small. This transformation occurs from the inside out—not the other way around.

The transition process demands skills we may not have been previously taught or in which we have not yet gained experience. Hence it is characterized by the acquisition of new knowledge and skills, which we discover for ourselves or acquire from a trained counsellor.

Such a career transition requires that we try to foretell the immediate future, and this has to be done in an environment where economies, social systems, and the nature of employment are undergoing rapid structural change. The traditional benchmarks we acquired during our adolescence and early adulthood have either vanished, been eroded, or shifted. At best our career planning is a calculated "guesstimate," hence the need to develop alternative options for our career action steps.

Once we have mastered our career transition, we face the future more confidently. The unexpected life events are likely to be welcomed, not feared, or at the least better managed.

Career transitions, however painful and disorienting, are pathways for growth, new learning, and discovery. We gain a new inner wisdom. We achieve a purging of some or all of the dragging anchors of the past and feel less fettered, though still mindful that future career transitions need to accommodate the needs of others close to us. We feel pride in our accomplishment yet often are humble about the experience. We acknowledge that life is really an exciting journey.

Bibliography and Useful Further Reading

Baxter, Janeen. *Work at Home,* University of Queensland Press, Brisbane, 1993.

Brim, Gilbert. *Ambition: How We Manage Success and Failure Throughout Our Lives,* Basic Books (division of HarperCollins Publishers), New York, 1992.

Doak, James. *Coming to Life: The Emergence of Self in the Human Life Cycle,* (new edition), Blue Dolphin Publishing, Nevada City, California, 1993.

Goman, Carol. *Adapting to Change,* Crisp Publications, USA, 1992.

Hudson, Frederick M. *The Adult Years: Mastering the Art of Self Renewal,* Jossey-Bass Publishers, San Francisco, 1991.

Kinder, H. and Ginsberg, M. *Stress Training For Life,* Wright Books, Melbourne, 1990.

Kineldorf, Martin. *Serious Play: A Workbook about Leisure Wellness,* Ten Speed Press, Berkeley, California, 1994.

Levinson, David. *The Seasons of a Man's Life,* Knopf, New York, 1978.

Merriam, Sharan B. and Clark, M. Carolyn. *Lifelines: Patterns of Work, Love and Learning in Adulthood,* Jossey-Bass Publishers, San Francisco, 1991

Saltzman, Amy. *Downshifting: Reinventing Success on a Slower Track,* HarperCollins, New York, 1992.

Silverstein, Lisa. *Dual Career Marriage,* Lawrence Erlbaum Associates, New Jersey, 1992.

Sinetar, Marsha. *Do What You Love, The Money Will Follow,* Dell Publishing, New York, 1989.

Sinetar, Marsha. *A Way Without Words: A Guide for Spiritually Emerging Adults,* Paulist Press, Mahwah, New Jersey, 1992.

Spencer, Sabina A. and Adams, John D. *Life Changes: Growing Through Personal Transitions,* Impact Publishers, California, 1990.

Super, D.E. "A life-span, life-space approach to career development" (pp. 197-261), in D. Brown, L. Brooks and Assoc. (Eds), *Career Choice and Development: Applying contemporary theories to practice,* (2nd edition), Jossey-Bass Publishers, San Francisco, 1990.

PART 2

Managing Worklife Transitions

. . . .

- Personal responsibility
- Willingness to risk
- Data gathering
- Stimulus questions
- Self-help
- Help from others
- The real facts about goals
- The obstacles of time
- Our inner self
- Biographical review
- Structured analysis
- A formula for worklife satisfaction
- Bibliography and useful further reading

. . . .

. . . .

At the highest level of self-realization the distinction between work and life disappears. Your real life doesn't start after five and on weekends. The secret is that work is really an opportunity to play adult games with real money, real resources and real people. When what you do coincides with who you are, you can have it all.

Susan Jacoby, *The Possible She*
(Farrar, Straus and Giroux, 1979)

A career is a time-extended working out of a purposeful life pattern through work undertaken by the individual.

National Vocational Guidance Association
USA, 1973

A career is one's progress through life.

Funk and Wagnell Dictionary, USA

Transition (tran sizh un) n. Passage or change from one place, state, or action to another; change, change-over, passing, passage, shifting, jump, leap, conversion, creation, transformation, transmutation; progression, gradation, graduation.

(Budget Macquarie Dictionary)
Australian Edition

. . . .

Personal Responsibility

I have a good idea, and then think of a million reasons why I can't do it.

We didn't ask to be born or to whom. Yet now we are here it's common sense to make the best of life's journey. How we do this is in our own hands. It's a matter of good self-management and to leave it to the elusiveness of luck is unwise. If fortunate events help us along, that's a bonus. Just as we take out insurance to guard against the unpredictable, so personal career review and goal setting strengthens our resourcefulness in coping with the unexpected and non-events (i.e., those that were anticipated but did not occur). Skills and strategies for managing our career and personal self **can** be learned. It is not being personally responsible to say to oneself, "I can't. I shouldn't." Or, as John Greenleaf Whittier expressed it: "Of all sad words of tongue or pen, the saddest are these: 'It might have been.' "

Our personal identity is related to our goals. This means that as we search for our worklife goals we are also searching for our real self. Lacking a sufficiently clear and detailed self-assessment, people often put themselves in new situations no better suited to them than previous ones. They are, in fact, experimenting by trial and error. It is much more satisfactory to learn how to develop a vision of the kind of job content, employment environment, and lifestyle you should be seeking than be diverted into "interesting" opportunities which do not really suit. The answer to our inner well-being cannot come simply from responding to enticing recruitment advertisements or from the persuasive tone of a consultant from an employment agency. A thorough self-assessment, which I call a three-dimensional analysis, is required. Figure 8 illustrates this.

"I do not get any recognition from my boss for what I do," is the most common reason I hear for dissatisfaction with work, whether from participants in a workshop or a client in counselling. These people are failing to acknowledge two things: one, that one's self-evaluation is many times more important than the opinion of others; and, two, that they would not need the acknowledgment of their efforts from others so much if they analyzed what it is they want to do in a job and the criteria for measuring their effectiveness and personal growth within it. Time and time again I notice that people have a way of siding against

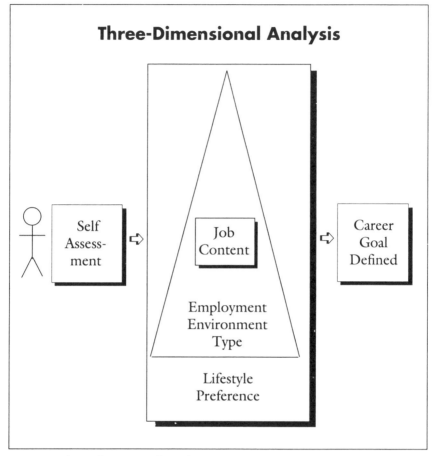

Figure 8. Three-dimensional Analysis.

themselves. They align themselves with the appraisal of others. Their self-worth in their career situation is dependent on the opinion of people with whom they work. This is a sign that the person has done insufficient self-analysis to determine real worklife needs and identify his or her own self-concept.

What we need to do is learn more about how to strengthen ourselves from within—not discount our own perceptions of how we are doing when others voice an opinion or we interpret their lack of feedback negatively.

We are responsible for the degree of satisfaction we feel. There are always options available if we are willing to take charge of our lives and set out to improve things. There are always ways to overcome obstacles and constraints. By setting worklife goals we are not only meeting our own responsibility for life management but also demonstrating to others that it is a worthwhile activity. The value to our partner—the significant other—in our lives, our children, those we care about, is hard to assess precisely, but few would deny that there is some residual benefit conveyed to them through our example when we accept personal responsibility for our career satisfaction and take the steps necessary to achieve it. The result is often a better relationship within the home.

> . . . this is the beauty of choosing the right livelihood. As people honor the actions they value most—by doing them—they become more authentic, more reliable, more self-disciplined. They grow to trust themselves more; they listen to their inner voice as a steady, truthful and strengthening guide for what to do next and how to do it.
>
> Marsha Sinetar in
> *Do What You Like, The Money Will Follow*
> (Dell/Bantam, 1989)

· · · · · · · · · ·

All the separate achievements in a period of career reassessment combined to produce in me a profound, personal revolution; together they built self-esteem and a sense of direction for my life. I grew, or pushed myself, out of a life pattern of depression, lassitude, and anxiety—my greatest achievement of my life to date.

· · · · · · · · · ·

Willingness to Risk

*Career analysis has taught me that when I find the courage
to say what I want, I discover the way to get it.*

Managing a worklife transition is about identifying the risks which are
worth taking. Our past provides us with examples of both inappropriate and worthwhile risk-taking actions. It takes hard work to remember, evaluate, and reflect on the results which occurred and the knowledge we have gained from taking such risks. Whatever trauma we have
experienced in the past in our education, personal life, or previous
employment, it is important to recognize that it can distort our ability
to focus on the present and future. It is likely that others will refer
frequently to our past, particularly selection interviewers, promotion
panels or managers at career appraisal reviews. The possibility of disap-
pointment or rejection by others does exist and can never be fully eliminated. An important career direction change can make us apprehensive
about the inherent risks. A mentor of mine in the past said to me just
once, yet powerfully, "Change is normal. It's evidence that you are still
breathing."

Risks in your career change can be substantially reduced by acquiring sufficient information to make wise career decisions. Information
about yourself and facts about job prospects and employment environments needs to be gathered in a thorough, systematic manner.

Being unemployed provides you with an opportunity for self-exploration. To be able to observe the world of work, listen to and question others, arrange information interviews, explore skills and training
demands of differing occupations, are investigative actions about
work options which can improve your decision making and career planning. Generally viewed as socially undesirable, a period of unemploy-
ment does provide time for reflection and reorientation. You may
never before in your life have examined the issue of your worklife
so thoroughly. To make the best use of this time, you need to be self-
motivated, prepared to risk by experiment, able to approach strangers,
and ready to try to make sense of a myriad of information, some
conflicting.

Data Gathering

*The most amazing things have happened since mid-August.
The first two days were filled with elation; I felt cut free from
self-imposed chains of confusion and despair—but I was soon
reminded of the old saying, "What goes up must come down,"
and I hit Earth with a thud.*

*I journeyed through waves of absolute terror. As I began to
gather data my mind went completely blank (shock, horror,
confusion). This went on for a week, and I now see that it
was caused by the very action of doing something about my
stagnation, depression, dissatisfaction.*

*Slowly, I began to pick exercises that were easiest, and kept
up a steady pace until I had completed everything I felt I
needed to do. Finally, when I completed my list of "Skills
likely to be used in Future Employment" I knew that I had
made enormous progress. It fitted like a key to a lock.*

*I've moved to a new space internally and feel that I'm on
my way to some changes.*

Your journey of self-discovery is better taken methodically and slowly.
The challenge is to select what type of data is relevant and how it should
be collected. Finding out who you are today requires time, resources,
and quietness. When you do find out, you gain a new sense of identity,
self-esteem, and personal power. Self-assessment is an act of self-love.
Other people may criticize the process as being selfish, but unless you
search for the unique person you have become—by identifying your
special gifts, or skills—you will not know how to be fruitfully selfless
and contribute to the well-being of others.

It is easy to become a perpetual student of self and worklife options,
however for most of us the need to make career decisions is thrust
upon us, with little luxury of time in which to decide how to act or
evaluate alternatives. We often need to make compromises in such situations. Do the best we can in the data-gathering process and then implement what appears expedient. A procedure, or sequence, for data gathering is necessary to prevent hasty decisions and so reduce the likelihood of a career action that doesn't produce the desired results.

An approach which reduces risks is structured analysis—a method
by which you can gather and record data, extract trends, themes, and

key factors in an orderly manner. This approach is well suited to developing an understanding of how you make important life decisions and plans. It requires that you first pay considerable attention to assessing who you are today and how you have developed over a period of time. A saying which initially can sound trite is actually valid: the answer to your future lies in your past. This longitudinal approach enables you to trace the influence of the past on your present. This provides insights into the motivations and activities that have led to how you feel and act in your worklife today, but also provides important clues for future directions for your career growth. Self-understanding, therefore, is the key to determining your career future.

There are a variety of data-gathering career-assessment methods, ranging from psychometric tests and interest inventories, which usually require a qualified person to feed back the interpretation to you, to analyses you can undertake entirely by yourself. My work over the past decade has focused on designing self-help methods which people can use. They take the form of a combination of an autobiographical review and a series of stimulus questions contained within sets of questionnaires. The self-assessment method does not necessarily require the assistance of another person to interpret it before the information can be used and applied to career choice and career management.

The biographical review approach enables you to gain self-knowledge through writing about major events in your life and the ways in which you have dealt with these experiences. Insights into your latent skills or talents can be acquired and trends and themes in your development and behaviors can be detected. Such data is essential to informed career planning. I will expand later in this book on the biographical review approach.

Stimulus Questions

Stimulus questions are found in a series, or set, of questionnaires which break down the process of gathering data for each stage of career review, decision making, planning, and implementation. Stimulus questions enable you to gather data about what is relevant to your career decision making and discard what is not. They are asked in a carefully determined order and provoke reflections, analysis, and opinion form-

Stimulus Questionnaires

Characteristics

- Provide structured review of relevant factors for career decisions
- Prompt data which may otherwise be missed or ignored
- Record data which has practical applications
- Require memory search and self-honesty
- Usually improve self-esteem
- Are completed at own pace and in privacy
- Make order of an otherwise confusing array of data
- Provide the comfort of acting rather than being passive about one's career fate

Samples of Stimulus Questions

- What work tasks and skills usage do I really enjoy?
- What kind of activities cause me to be so involved that I lose track of time?
- What do I avoid or put off doing though I have the training and experience for the activities?
- What seven or eight words sum up the way I approach problem solving?
- With what kind of work colleagues do I work best?
- In retrospect, list career accomplishments which you regard as most worthwhile?
- What makes me feel really good when I do it well?
- What new learning appeals to me most over the next three years?
- What working conditions have stimulated me to produce well?
- In what work situations have I been at my most innovative?

Figure 9. Stimulus Questionnaires.

ing. They help you make coherent sense of the myriad of facts and events in your life to date. Your responses to each set of stimulus questions contribute to the various stages of data gathering essential to risk-reducing career planning.

As you progress through questionnaires with the characteristics described in Figure 9, you are learning through doing, expanding your awareness of options and forming personal resolutions. You undertake them alone—in privacy—as a form of homework. You can proceed with your responses at your own pace. Stimulus questions like those in Figure 9 do not lead you directly to a list of occupations on which to base your career decisions. You are guided to initiate your own career exploration and develop detective, communication, and research skills which enable you to carry out the task of matching your requirements with types of occupations and employment environments.

Some people experience difficulty with self-search exercises of this nature. They may want a speedy resolution to their problem, a quick fix. Some will not experiment adequately with such questionnaires before concluding that they do not need them or that this method is unappealing. Reluctance to commit personal thoughts in writing—even private notes—will deter others. If you experience these obstacles, it is common sense to seek out a career counsellor who can introduce alternative methods of resolving your particular career problem.

Those who take to the stimulus questions method acquire the value of feeling more in charge of their career direction and, as they progress through them, their self-confidence inevitably rises. They become confident that their diligence will bring the results they deserve for undertaking the effort. Their motivation to see the task through to a satisfying conclusion usually soars.

Unless there is a real commitment to change or to take the actions necessary to achieve an improvement in your worklife, neither the stimulus questions nor the biographical review method is useful. Another barrier is trying to make critical life management or major career decisions after only small amounts of data gathering. Skimping on the task, avoiding responding to stimulus questions that require deep thought and decisiveness will not produce adequate results. It may take many weeks of strenuous effort before effective decisions and workable plans can be formulated. Figure 10 outlines the benefits of this method.

This amount of effort can itself be a deterrent. The motivation to

Stimulus Questions Method

Possible Benefits

- Inspires self-help among those with concerns about career issues

- Guarantees your participation—you don't just read the material, you "do it"

- Helps you cope with issues that can be handled only by you

- Will appeal to you if you prefer to analyze important issues about yourself privately

- You can consider and make judgments and choices over a period of time

- Facilitates your focusing on what is really important in work and life management

- Enables you to identify what is your responsibility and what is another's, such as an employer's, concerning your career development

- Helps you to identify where help is needed from others

- Is useful as "homework" before or between counselling sessions with a career adviser

- Is a time-saving resource, as published questionnaire materials exist for you to follow

- Reduces the career hazard of demanding from your employer career development support which is neither appropriate nor adequately justifiable

- Helps you prepare requests for your manager in his or her career coaching role

Figure 10. Stimulus Questions Method.

change current circumstances needs to be strong. It demands self-discipline, fortitude, and patience to be thorough through the data-gathering stages. The process is self-evaluative. It requires courage to see ourselves as we really are and like the result.

In my book, *Stop Postponing the Rest of Your Life* (Ten Speed Press, 1993), I have published 54 questionnaires containing stimulus questions. There are a further series of stimulus questionnaires in another book of mine, *Your Career Planner: Reducing the Risks to Those Worth Taking.* In most major bookstores there are several alternative titles containing questionnaires devised for the same purpose—in other words, to facilitate the self-exploration process of people determined to help themselves. I have listed some of these titles in the Appendix at the conclusion of this book. But choose carefully. Many self-help books containing career planning questionnaires are too narrow in scope or gloss over issues and steps that may be critical to a successful self-help process.

Self-help

In undertaking self-assessment and proceeding through to implementing career planning decisions, we assume sole responsibility for helping ourselves. Self-help fosters feelings of "ownership." It's my data; it's my life. This increases the probability that the gathered information will be used and acted upon. But herein lies a caution: assuming a self-help responsibility for our own career management can be taken beyond the point of being useful. Self-assessment demands introspection, self-evaluation, and reflection, as well as determination. But there are important data elements that lie outside ourselves. To gain the perspectives of others about our behaviors, how we are perceived, how we use our skills, and of our specific situation requires that we seek out the opinions of others. Others may be usefully recruited to assist us in interpreting our data gathering in the self-assessment phase. They are likely to be very useful in adding insights into various ways that the data we have gathered can be applied. It is important in our career management to know when to say self-help and when to say "help." In my experience, which is, by nature of my profession, the experiences of my career transition clients, I see many examples of the usefulness of the brief intervention of another. It can bring about considerable in-sights and improved self-knowledge, which can be used in meaningful ways to form useful conclusions, make effective plans, and make decisions.

The first writer of advice about career choice, Frank Parsons, ac-knowledged this need for the counsel of others when he wrote in *Choosing a Vocation* (Houghton Mifflin, 1909):

> The building of a career is quite as difficult a problem as the build-ing of a house, yet few ever sit down with pen and pencil, with expert information and counsel, to plan a working career and deal with the life problem scientifically, as they would deal with the problem of building a house, taking the advice of an architect to help them.

The need for gathering information through consultation with others has never been so urgent as when you are intent on being more in charge of your worklife direction.

Help from Others

When working hard to advance a career the need often arises to have someone to talk with about our feelings and behavior. In most cases, we would feel inhibited talking to our boss because of a natural reluc-tance to share too much of ourselves with a person who represents the power to advance or suppress our career ambitions.

We all need help from another person to bring out our best perfor-mance, a person with whom we can share our hopes and disappoint-ments in an unfettered way, who can review the proposed next step in our personal career management program.

A good coach is regarded as essential for improving the perfor-mance of an athlete. The value of coaches is that they are not directly involved in the activity. Coaches can observe the performance and iden-tify the critical areas requiring refinement. The next step is to provide feedback to the athlete in a manner that brings about a change in be-havior and an improvement in the result.

The coach, or mentor, you select should be a person you can trust—someone with whom you can be open and who is willing to be frank with you. Remember, you are not necessarily looking for a friend. You are seeking another person as a counsellor who will help you manage your own career rather than leave it to chance.

A mentor is someone we feel drawn to and from whom we can learn. When we are faced with a decision concerning our careers and behavior at work we are commencing a new transition. A transition requires us to identify the options, select one appropriate to our particular circumstances and move purposely to implement the appropriate steps to conclude the transition successfully. We may need to change mentors when the nature of career transition differs. A person able to advise us on one issue may not be suitable for a different transition. Figure 11 describes some of the possible issues a mentor can help you explore.

A good mentor will help you to see not only the options and tasks before you but also the broader context that gives a focus to those tasks. Having a mentor is not a passive process of just listening to advice. You need to question, debate, submit proposals, and prepare for discussions with your mentor. Unless you do, your mentor cannot help with three distinct types of assistance. These are to support, to challenge, and to provide vision.

In **supporting** us, mentors show that they have empathy with our problem and personal situation. They listen, inspire trust over what we

---

A Mentor Helps . . .

- Provide risk-free discussions on ideas

- Assess the reality of your career action plan

- Make use of networks and information resources

- You initiate appropriate career transition activities

- You recognize abilities and limitations

- By recommending effective behavior and strategies

Figure 11. A Mentor Helps . . .

are sharing, and help us define the boundaries within which decisions are to be made. Their role as **challengers** to our ideas is to introduce contradictory views, question the basis of our opinions and the perspective we have on the problem. They may decline to answer our questions directly in the best interests of being of help to us.

As we progress on to the stage where **vision** is provided, the mentor reassures us that the career transition can be made, helps us define what will signify success, and provides an insight as to the potential rewards gained from the resolution of our particular dilemma.

A good mentor is not there to provide the answers but to assist us to develop our skills at resolving career-related complications. To demand "Which way should I go?" is improper use of a mentor relationship.

Our literary heritage provides many expressions of this form of companionship. My favorite is by George Eliot, the pseudonym of Mary Ann Evans: "Oh the comfort, the inexpressible comfort, of feeling safe with a person, having neither to weigh thoughts nor measure words, but to pour them all out, just as it is, chaff and grain together, knowing that a faithful ally will take and sift them, keeping what is worth keeping, and then, with the breath of kindness, blowing the rest away."

In order to commit your personal thoughts to another in anticipation of constructive advice you need to have confidence in the skill, knowledge, and ethics of your mentor. You must be sure that he or she has the credentials to help you before you start communicating. The relationship must be reciprocal to be sustained. You must, by your subsequent actions, reflect your mentor's own qualities, contribute to that person's need for self-esteem, and communicate pleasure in the sharing of wisdom. The mentor must facilitate the development of your own decisions—not dictate your actions.

Whether the relationship with your mentor is short or lasts a long time, it should never be one of dependency. It is a relationship for **mutual** planning and **mutual** negotiation. As you both focus on one or more worklife problems you have raised, your mentor advises you and makes recommendations. You should not, however, abdicate your responsibility for making your own resolutions and for deciding how to act. It's your worklife. It's you who must implement the decisions. Your mentor suggests, checks your reasoning, and provides encouragement.

Your aim should not be to please, but to learn from your mentor; not to avoid questions, but to ask them; not to hide mistakes, but to discuss what can be learned from them; not to conceal information, but to share it; not to be protected, but to be encouraged to take new risks.

To avoid misunderstandings, make your expectations explicit. Let your needs be known. Let your mentor know how the relationship is meeting your needs. Share what you are feeling and why.

Choose from Figure 12 which of the five career stages you are currently experiencing. Read the advice and plan what action you will take to identify an appropriate mentor.

When you have identified your mentor, you may both want to complete the questionnaire in Figure 13 and discuss your responses.

Career Stages
Where Mentors Are Useful

Action: Check your first choice. Then complete the section that follows on that choice.

		Your Choice
1.	Career Awareness Stage	☐
2.	Career Preparation Stage	☐
3.	Career Orientation Stage	☐
4.	Career Expansion Stage	☐
5.	Career Advancement Stage	☐

Figure 12. Career Stages Where Mentors Are Useful.

1. Career Awareness Stage

Support and information needs

You may be about to:

- choose an educational institution for study ☐
- accept a new job offer ☐
- establish a small business ☐
- change careers or relocate ☐

Mentors can help you consider the realities ahead so that an informed selection can be made.

Source of mentors

Seminar/workshop leaders, former students, employment agency consultants, small business advisory services, career counsellors, chambers of commerce, people who are in the field of work you are considering.

People you now have in mind to contact:

_____

_____

_____

_____

_____

Figure 12 (continued).

2. Career Preparation Stage

Support and information needs

To be in this stage, you have selected the direction of your career transition. I'm clearly in this stage: Yes/No. Adjusting to new learning and new environments is often difficult. A mentor can help you to:

• Assess tutoring, counselling services, or more experienced students (**as a student**)

• find out information about the employer which cannot be learned by carrying out job tasks (**as a new employee**)

Source of mentors

Personnel staff, designated mentors provided by the employer, work colleagues, your manager.

People you now have in mind to contact:

_____

_____

_____

_____

_____

_____

_____

Figure 12 (continued).

3. Career Orientation Stage

Support and information needs

In this stage, you have completed your transition into meaningful work. To secure the cooperation of your new work colleagues requires intuitive solutions to immediate problems. To become competent you need to do more than apply your knowledge to the job. You must earn the right to feel welcomed and respected.

Mentors can assist your understanding of the employer's culture, the norms of behavior, how to obtain help from others.

Source of mentors

Professional associations, human resource personnel, employees with longer service.

People you have in mind to contact:

_____

_____

_____

_____

_____

_____

_____

Figure 12 (continued).

4. Career Expansion Stage

Support and information needs

At intervals you should consider your career path options. When you do this, you are in the career expansion stage. Frequently the scarcity of information hinders a comprehensive evaluation of alternatives. Mentors can help provide this information or recommend sources where it can be found. Their advice can facilitate:

* preparation of your plans for self-development

* expansion of your talent

* improvement of your eligibility for consideration

Source of mentors

Subject area interest groups, proven professionals, acquaintances in the same industry.

People you have in mind to contact:

_____

_____

_____

_____

_____

_____

_____

Figure 12 (continued).

5. Career Advancement Stage

Support and information needs

Once you have chosen your career path option, you need to determine how and to whom you should present your case for what you seek and why you merit it. Yes, this is me! Yes/No

Those who have traversed this career stage represent the best source of mentors with whom to discuss strategies, documentation, and communication methods. You seek their counsel for a specified utilitarian purpose.

Source of mentors

Your manager, personnel staff, senior members of your profession who work for other employers, successful role models, executives, institutes of management.

People you have in mind to contact:

_____

_____

_____

_____

_____

_____

_____

_____

Figure 12 (continued).

Mentor Relationship Questionnaire

Action: When you identify your mentors, you can both complete this questionnaire and discuss your responses:

Circle the number you consider the most accurate:

1 = Strongly agree   4 = Disagree
2 = Agree   5 = Strongly disagree
3 = Maybe, not certain

Networking does not mean talking only to important people who have senior jobs.   1 2 3 4 5

I maintain a list of useful contacts and acquaintances to help me in readiness for when I need to network for information.   1 2 3 4 5

Career pathfinding is different from networking.   1 2 3 4 5

I participate in the activities of my professional association.   1 2 3 4 5

I send Christmas cards to my business contacts.   1 2 3 4 5

A mentor must not be the same sex as the seeker of assistance.   1 2 3 4 5

Both men and women are increasingly finding it helpful to use mentors in their careers.   1 2 3 4 5

The age of the mentor does not matter.   1 2 3 4 5

It is ethical to change mentors if I believe there are no longer benefits.   1 2 3 4 5

It is okay to have a mentor who works for the same employer.   1 2 3 4 5

Usually the higher the mentor's position the more the mentor can do for me.   1 2 3 4 5

Figure 13. Mentor Relationship Questionnaire.

The relationship between a male mentor and a woman can be more complex than a woman-to-woman relationship.	1 2 3 4 5
A counsellor can also serve as a mentor.	1 2 3 4 5
When I have a tough problem to resolve I should involve my mentor.	1 2 3 4 5
My mentor does not have to have the same personality traits as me.	1 2 3 4 5
The best mentor has a wide range of current skills to pass on.	1 2 3 4 5
A mentor provides more than friendship.	1 2 3 4 5
The primary purpose of a mentor is to be an adviser in my personal development.	1 2 3 4 5

Figure 13 (continued).

The Real Facts About Goals

I list and document just about everything I do. How I surf and train, what I eat, when I go to bed and wake up. It takes me ages to make a decision, but when I do it is the right one because I go through such a rigid process to get there.

World Surfing Champion, Barton Lynch

Self-assessment can lapse into a form of self-indulgence unless it leads to something useful and personally nurturing. The real objective of deciding upon self-help, gathering data about self, and using a mentor is to provide a base from which career directions can be clarified. Plans can then be developed so that goals can be achieved within specific time schedules.

We may hesitate about making worklife goals for several reasons. Our record in the past may indicate that it has been a waste of time; events over which we had no control took over and stopped them being fulfilled. The demands on our time by others may give us little hope that, having set goals, we will be able to implement them. Making a living, attending to family needs, caring for others, commuting, surviving in our job, managing staff and work in progress, keeping the boss happy, and many other factors crowd our waking hours.

Despite all these inhibitors, it is an established fact that people who set well-thought-out goals convey an aura of purpose in their life, project themselves more confidently, and smile more. Goals helped them to identify obstacles in advance and to solve problems encountered along the way.

What makes them so different? What secrets of goal setting have they discovered? Whether by research, experimentation, training, or by chance, they have learned how to set realizable goals. The secrets are not very mysterious or complicated. In fact, they are:

- Goals must be your very own.
- Goals must be written down.
- Goals must be consistent with your values, interests, and abilities.
- Goals must be clearly defined so you know when they are reached.
- Goals must be both short-term and long-term.
- Goals must be realistic and attainable.
- Goals must be thought through to their consequences.
- Reinforcement for goal-achieving behavior must be planned and scheduled; this should take the form of personal rewards to mark each stage of achievement.

Remember, goals don't have to be new. It is quite appropriate for someone setting worklife goals to include certain activities they enjoy doing now, so that they are sure to allow time for them in the future.

· · · · · · · · · ·

Why do I want to change careers? I wanted my "old" career, but once you accomplish what you set out to do, it's often not what it is cut out to be—so I will just let go of it.

· · · · · · · · · ·

Research into why people do achieve informs us that achievers believe their efforts will make a difference to their lives, they take on responsibility for their own behavior, they establish moderate-risk goals. Setting a goal beyond one's reach can only lead to frustration and a decline in self-esteem.

A thorough assessment of where one is at the present time is essential before establishing goals and career directions. Factors such as the economy, labor market nuances, growth and restraints in different industries, and supply and demand fluctuations in occupations all have a bearing on whether career goals are realizable. It is therefore important to include contingency plans and goal options in your career planning.

· · · · · · · · · ·

This isn't just about changing jobs but facing up to who I am and the realities around that.

· · · · · · · · · ·

The Obstacles of Time

The further we progress in a career and, perhaps, extend family responsibilities, the less time there seems to be to evaluate whether we are going in the right direction. It is also essential to take time to appraise whether we are with the most appropriate employer for furthering our career. In fact, in a busy worklife, time has probably come to seem the greatest obstacle to accomplishing many things that are important to our inner well-being—not only the management of a career.

For too many, decisions about career actions are taken in a hurry. The lure of a recruitment advertisement, an enticement from an employment agency, or a disappointing performance review from the boss all too frequently precipitate the decision to change employment circumstances.

It is a shame that many of us feel guilty about taking time to contemplate the quality of our work and way of life. Many feel that this is a form of self-indulgence—a selfish act—and, for this reason, unhealthy. How many worklife problems would be solved and how great an increase to career satisfaction would there be if more individuals could find the courage to reduce their daily commitments, allocate time for self, and process their thoughts before resuming with the hectic pace of modern-day work activities?

To deal effectively with a career transition we need to pause regularly and take stock. Many of us do not take this pause. As individuals we are often uncomfortable in changed, unbalanced situations and quickly seek to reduce the discomfort we experience. We often take the first job offer made if we are out of work. In the face of a loss of inner identity previously obtained from a job or career path attached to a particular employer, and with the future we anticipated within it abruptly gone, we are prone to act hastily in attempting to replace what we have lost. The sense of self, fractured by our external world, needs healing before rational decision making can take place. But rarely do we give this a chance to take place. In a desire to end the discomfort of the present phase as soon as possible, we accept any option available to us. But that precious commodity, time, is essential if we are to manifest our true self in our future worklife.

Any self-assessment process requires a great deal of time, energy, and discipline. Career and personal self-review should not be rushed. The answers which occur quickly are often not the most valid or the most useful.

· · · · · · · · · ·

My change has been worth it. I know myself much better than I did. I've learned that my personal resources, my own strength and capacity to hang in, are greater than I'd ever realized.

· · · · · · · · · ·

Our Inner Self

Each of us has an individual world that has been created around our view of self. This inward view of ourselves gives each of us a personal perspective on the world around us. The events occurring in the outside world, whether work, family, or other happenings, are interpreted in accordance with the current state of our inner world or view of self. Some call this inner world our self-concept. Just as events are occurring outside us—a continual series of changes—so too our inner world is changing. Our view of these external events, therefore, changes as our sense of self changes and our inward view is modified accordingly.

The true nature of our career—that is, its meaning for our inner world—may not be the same for those who observe us, whether they are our loved ones, boss, counsellors, employment consultants, or relatives. For example, if we are promoted at work, others are likely to view this event as an indicator of success. But inwardly we may view it as costing dearly in terms of our desire to have more time for personal projects of a non-work nature. Being retrenched may appear to others as a setback while our inner self may feel relief that we no longer work in a particular set of work situations.

· · · · · · · · · ·

I have discovered that a good job is secondary to a good life. Enjoyment comes from yourself and from your attitudes to job and life, not just from what you do for a living.

· · · · · · · · · ·

The way in which our inner self responds to these interacting external and internal forces determines the form our career—in fact, our life—will take. The choices, decisions, and emotional investments we make in work, family, and other activities shape the overall nature of our way of life. Because neither we nor the environment stay still, changes in both will influence, alter, and sometimes disturb our viewpoint. Both major and minor changes can disrupt the balance. A redefinition of self and the external world is required in order to restore comfort in the way we live and to be sure that the actions we take are really right for us. New assessments, an expanded awareness of our strengths, skills, preferences, and values need to be made. Our career, then, is a sequence of alternating stable and transitional phases.

· · · · · · · · · ·

What I was not expecting from career assistance was the extent to which I have achieved insights into my own personality and behavior . . . plus the amazing variety of factors of relevance to my work satisfaction. It has not always been a comfortable experience, reawakening as it did previous and suppressed information. On the other hand, self-esteem has been raised by the identification of positive characteristics and lifestyle factors which have been taken entirely for granted.

· · · · · · · · · ·

Biographical Review

One of the techniques for self-assessment is a biographical review. The self-assessment technique of biographical review involves writing down a thorough account of most of your worklife experiences and other life events. It is, in effect, a retrospective diary. For centuries individuals have found it useful to write out an account of things that have taken place, and their feelings and decisions. It is a well proven method of moving to greater self-awareness, expanding creativity, and providing a focus for making important decisions. It provides the writer with a great deal of personal power. It also provides any person engaged in helping and supporting the career choices with a review of the essential data on which to base such assistance. It is reasonable to claim that people make career decisions not at an isolated moment but in the context of a lifetime of experiences, whether aged 17, 35, or 68. Elements of the past contribute to the current career situation and the difficulties being experienced and affect what will be the personal resources and perceived constraints on possible solutions.

The biographical review is a technique designed to help you analyze your capabilities and preferences in order to plan for a more fulfilling worklife. Those that undertake it need to be prepared to work very hard. The method is thorough and consequently takes considerable time. There will be times when you will be tempted to skip over a step or to be less than conscientious when completing one. The value you gain is very much affected by how much time, effort, and self-honesty are devoted to each step of the process.

It is best to establish a steady pace of so much writing time per day, so many hours per week. It is unwise to set aside a whole day to think and write. Such sustained personal review is exhausting and may distort the recordings.

Most of us learn, really learn, from our own experiences—not simply from having things happen to us but from reflecting on what happens so that the meaning of our experiences becomes clear and we can make choices based on our growing awareness rather than unchallenged assumptions. The positive and negative outcomes can be analyzed. We can make choices based on this reflection and analysis. Career action steps can be evolved which are based on these facts: *facts* because they did occur. Career planning based on assumptions does not have a valid foundation. Hence, people in a career transition situation need to go back in time before they can progress into the future in an assured way. As we become certain of the basis upon which we are planning, our confidence in achieving successful outcomes will naturally grow. The subsequent course of action you take to improve your career cannot be guaranteed to produce consistent worklife satisfaction, but it can be confined to the risks that are worth taking . . . not haphazard ones.

Biographical review puts us in touch with where we are today. Once grasped and accepted, these data can help us determine where we want to be. None of this is new wisdom. Confucius, for one, identified this process many centuries ago. It is not sufficient to think earnestly about our past. This thinking must be accompanied by writing down our thoughts. Our thinking needs to be guided along certain paths, otherwise we can become angry, resentful, even despairing.

Your biographical writings are likely to begin tentatively and self-consciously. As you experiment with different styles of recording, you will become more comfortable, and words will soon come faster than you can write them down. Some prefer to write in complete sentences, others in list form. I have noticed that those who record on many small cards find it easier to rearrange the information into broad categories or major findings when the writing is completed. Such writing provides a safe place to record what you think about yourself, your work and the events that have been significant to date in your journey through life. Through the writings you do as part of your biographical review, you will become aware of how you have been changing and growing, moving through phases and crossroads. You will see the effect they have on your current outlook. You can gain a new sense of confidence, which is necessary before you proceed to think through and find creative solutions to your worklife dilemmas.

The writing process suits many of us who prefer to think slowly and carefully about matters which are very important to us. We don't have to defend ourselves to others while we write. We can make spelling, syntactical, or grammatical mistakes and it doesn't matter a damn. The *content* of what we are writing is what is important!

Many people have commented to me that writing a worklife review is like getting in touch with one's inner self. As they record their experiences, they can check earlier decisions and evaluate their feelings about people, situations, and employment environments. We invest power in the things on which we focus when writing, so I encourage my clients to concentrate on the happier moments of their worklife experiences and not to dwell too long on the negative. You should take frequent breaks from the task, but you should not procrastinate about returning to it, as the biographical review is a powerful means of realizing your own unique true potential.

Harnessing *new* technology can assist the whole process. If you are what is loosely called computer literate you can use a word processing program for this task. By scrolling forward and backwards you can add thoughts, considerations, queries at any stage. But you should not go back and change what you have written. If a skilled helper is to be engaged to facilitate the career transition, the counsellor needs to see the routes by which your thoughts are traveling. If you want to record more comments, you should simply add them along with a note that they reflect a later change in your thinking.

Once the biographical review is completed, it can give you new, and sometimes surprising, insights into self and its relation to your career and life management issues. It can also provide a structure to something of which you are already aware. As you review the things you have written, you will notice that realistic information and worthwhile clues will develop. They are realistic because the recording process has allowed you to incorporate thought, imagination, introspection, and feelings, along with facts about actual events and their logical analysis. Figure 14, the "Biographical Review Exercise," follows.

The adaptation of the biographical review technique to career analysis for adults occurred in the early seventies. A notable example is the elective tuition program for students within the Harvard MBA syllabus. This earned the Exxon award for the most creative course in business management in 1975. Nearby the late John C. Crystal was introducing the biographical review procedure to clients of his career transition counselling service based in New York. Richard Nelson Bolles worked with John in the design and publication of *Where Do I Go*

Biographical Review Exercise

Action: Remind yourself during this review that an important aspect of career analysis is directed at identifying tasks where you used the skills you have discovered you really have and enjoy using. The easiest trap is to look only at past job titles rather than the tasks and skills behind them. It is the tasks performed and skills used rather than the job title which provide or negate satisfaction in worklife.

- Every job, whatever its title, is made up of a set of tasks. Each of these tasks requires a number of skills. Your first activity is to identify *all* your skills by examining all the tasks you have carried out, whether at work or elsewhere, then those skills you *most like* using.

- Remember: skills are action-oriented words or statements that describe the function you were carrying out, e.g., public speaking, computing figures, organizing others, etc.

- Capabilities are personality traits like perseverance, honesty, etc., which describe the manner in which you applied these skills. Here are some examples: deeply concerned, enjoyed the challenge, earned respect, built a good team.

- Your search for these skills is for any evidence of ability, natural competence, proficiency, or personal quality you have demonstrated.

Step 1: Skills Assembly
Find your skills and capabilities using the following as a guide:

- Look over your biographical review and write down your total list of skills, e.g., writing, training/teaching others, etc.

- Reread every line, every sentence. Add to your list as additional skills reveal themselves.   *continued*

Figure 14. Biographical Review Exercise.

- Be wary of using generalized terms such as financial management: Was the skill used actually cost analysis, budget planning, or capital expenditure evaluations?

- Take several days over this exercise to allow your thoughts to crystallize. Aim to have a list of 70 skills within five days of beginning this analysis.

Remind yourself repeatedly that skills are action-oriented words or statements. Personal qualities or capabilities are traits which characterize a person. Skills, for which you are searching, may be one word descriptions or short sentences.

Step 2: Skills Classification

- Go back over your list of skills. Classify each skill by listing it under the particular skill most allied to it. Cross out from your original list as you transfer each one. New major skill headings or classifications will occur as you do this.

- Don't be concerned about listing a skill under more than one classification heading. This is likely to happen quite often.

Step 3: Skills Rating

- When all your skills and capabilities have been transferred to the new classifications, take each group in turn and read down each classification and mark with a (3) skills you know well and enjoy/enjoyed using. Put a (2) for skills you know well, but do not or did not enjoy very much. Put a (1) against those skills which you currently know little about using, but would like to know more.

- Put each classified group in order of preference by listing them according to the number of 3s you have rated the skills within each group. You arrive then at a point where you are much wiser about whether a career direction change is suggested and which occupations best suit your skills. It should be a

Figure 14 (continued).

pleasant surprise to note that each group is, in fact, a separate occupation—a new career—and is the proof that you can carry out the tasks involved within each one identified. At the same time you have assembled the data essential for an effective job search or promotion claim. The data can be used in a new résumé, job application letters, face-to-face selection interviews, performance review discussions, or career planning reviews with your manager.

Step 4: Review

- Go back over your total Biographical Review responses. Yes, one more time. The intention is to extract every single skill and capability that you have ever used and demonstrated. The more thoroughly you do this search, the more you will discover your personal uniqueness. And, therefore, the easier you will identify the most appropriate work content for you.

- You may need the help of another person to uncover all the skills. If you feel that you are stuck but believe more can be found, recruit a friend to review your data.

Figure 14 (continued).

From Here With My Life? (Ten Speed Press, 1974). Richard also wrote a companion title, *What Color Is Your Parachute?* (Ten Speed Press). Reprinted and updated every year since 1972, this book is referred to by most researchers and writers about career transitions. Both emphasize the importance and practicality of including biographical review in the self-assessment procedure.

. . . .

I do know that I will take from this writing experience a set of tools and a level of self-awareness (and sensitivity) that will undoubtedly have a profound impact upon my life.

. . . .

Structured Analysis

To provide a structure for the self-review, it is useful to employ a formula. Before proceeding to goal setting, it is necessary to form such a structure, so that our thinking is given a distinct focus and we can make sense of the complexities of our psychological makeup. The use of a formula helps us not only identify what is important within each aspect of our lives but also to determine how important each of these aspects is.

$$M + V + T - PC = Career\ Success$$

C. Brooklyn Derr, author of *Managing the New Careerists* (Jossey-Bass, 1989 edition), researched and developed a formula for helping people who sought his help in dealing with career confusion. The formula helps people to explore certain facts about themselves and to incorporate this information in a coherent way which will lead to improved understanding and comfort in choosing a particular career action. The formula comprises M for Motives, V for Values, T for Talents (or Skills or Competencies), PC for Perceived Personal Constraints.

- M = Motives—is about establishing our current primary wants.

- V = Values—helps focus on what a person values most. There are a variety of self-search aids to assist in sorting this out. One that I use in my counselling activities provides a choice of 41 individual values and requires that eight are selected as primary choices and ten as secondary choices.

  Our values do alter in peripheral ways from day to day but at our core these values are stable over the years. Most of our primary and secondary values will continue to guide our choices throughout our lives, but first we need to be clear on what our values truly are.

- T = Talents, skills, competencies. The search for all our skills and, in turn, for those we prefer to use is a major component of career analysis. Many researchers claim that each of us has more than 600 skills. In my experience I have seen this proven many times. Where the difficulty lies is in the individual's resistance to the hard work of identifying all of them. The first 25 are easy to identify. The next hundred are increasingly difficult. Certain skills may need to be "recruited" to assist in identifying the rest. In my opinion, Richard Nelson Bolles in *What Color Is Your Parachute?* provides the most thorough way to analyze this aspect of ourselves.

- PC = Perceived Personal Constraints. These feature in all of our lives. Listing them is important. Then the individual items can be examined in detail to determine the degree to which a constraint exists and a conclusion can be reached as to whether it really is an obstacle or can be circumnavigated by adopting a particular strategy or attitude.

Derr's formula is very useful in personal career decision making but is not sufficiently comprehensive to allow for all the information a person needs in making major work and life management decisions. Over the years I have developed a formula for taking people through the whole journey of self-exploration and evaluation of their options and on through to the successful implementation of their choice. In simplified form it is

$$SA + OA + DL + TT = \text{Worklife Satisfaction}$$

This provides a route for the personal journey of a detailed examination of the framework for personal career management and decision making. I call it structured analysis, and Figure 15 illustrates the process.

· · · · · · · · · ·

Since I've done this career analysis I see that I am my own person. I see that I have had courage in past career events and now know that I can use the same courage to make anything happen correctly for me from now on.

· · · · · · · · · ·

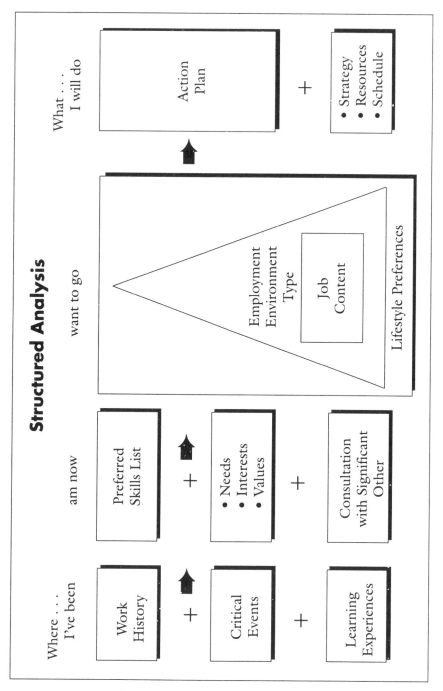

Figure 15. Structured Analysis.

A Formula for Worklife Satisfaction

Self-assessment and exploration proceed more comfortably if using a framework upon which lots of data can be fitted and viewed from different perspectives.

It is foolish to reinvent the wheel or ignore the wide variety of wheels that already exist. So the formula I have evolved incorporates the hard work of previous researchers and career development practitioners and their composite output of career decision-making approaches and systematic career counselling processes. But, like an artisan, I have added to and refined the wheels. I have rejected what has not worked to my standards of career support provision and discovered some nuts and bolts not previously invented. In particular, what I did discover was that many formulae designed to help a person neglected the difficulties of implementing a career action once it had been satisfactorily identified. I also found that several formulae researched and designed within an academic environment failed my tests when applied to the realities of the worklife situations of my clients. While originating in career development theory, my formula has an essentially practical approach which incorporates most, if not all, of the aspects of a person's work and way of life.

$$SA + ID + OA + DL + TT + TA = \text{Worklife Satisfaction}$$

By employing a structure to analyze our particular situation and put order into our thoughts and conclusions, we can then plan and carry out action steps to alter a worklife situation which is proving unsatisfactory. I have developed the structure $SA + ID + OA + DL + TT + TA$ over many years of helping others resolve their worklife difficulties, and I have refined it as I have observed my clients' journeys through it. It is a rational step-by-step approach which is not just an intellectual task but incorporates the emotional, cognitive, and psychological processes that involve the person as a whole and includes the environment in which he or she lives. An overview of this structure is provided in Figure 16.

A structure for our thinking and writing which will prevent us from dwelling unnecessarily on negative experiences is also required. The myriad of facts . . . experiences . . . of the life we have led in the past . . . need to be segmented. Clues may be buried in the depths of our memory, even our subconscious. A structure may prize them out into the open for considered review and for an evaluation of whether they should be incorporated in our career planning and subsequent career actions.

What follows has proved satisfactory to hundreds of people, though I am sure that as I continue to learn through my clients' experiences, the structure will undergo further refinement. I am conscious of the fact that because of the complexity of career management and life planning there are many variables affecting our worklife decisions that are as yet insufficiently explored.

You will remember from your school-day training in algebra and statistics that formulae are only useful once you have found the right data to put into the equation. To work out what data to put into the formula, let us look more closely at its components. The structure has six steps and within each step there are a number of activities. It is necessary to proceed through each of these discrete steps, in the sequence described. To change this sequence could jeopardize the validity and success of the outcomes

Now let's examine the formula SA + ID + OA + DL + TT + TA, and the activities within each step.

• *SELF-ASSESSMENT*

The first task is to assemble large volumes of disparate data and then deduce or infer from them patterns or trends from which conclusions can be drawn. The skill which is developed in this process is called inductive logic. To draw out the necessary information from your past, structured analysis stimulus questionnaires and the biographical review technique are used, and your responses recorded. Reflecting on the past, acting in the present, planning for the future all clearly suggest the fundamental process of learning through action. The action involved is to respond to stimulus questions, which lead you to examine each of the relevant features of your past and current way of life that have a bearing on your present worklife satisfaction on an inner level. It requires a systematic approach for thinking and recording information about your worklife and non-work activities. There are three parts to the assembly and interpretation of the self-assessment phase.

Overview of Worklife Satisfaction Formula

SA = Self-Assessment

Clarifying Issues and Concerns—Assembling an Information Base through Structured Analysis—Reviewing Current Job Effectiveness—Checking Employment Experiences—Abilities—Interests—Values—Primary Wants—Employment Environment Preferences—Lifestyle Considerations

ID = Interpreting Data

Analysis—Transferable Skills Identification—Developing Career Requirements—Resolving Ambiguities—Lifestyle Integration—Monetary Needs and Considerations—Barriers to Success—Identifying Perceived and Real Constraints

OA = Opportunity Awareness

Collecting Appropriate Information—Research—Gathering Information on Organizations—Reality Testing—Cultivating a Network—Mentoring—Evaluating Results—Selection of Career Action Options

DL = Decision Learning

Evaluating Career Action Options—Trade-offs—Deciding on Goals—Career Transition Scheduling

TT = Transition Training

Rehearsing for Negotiations—Documenting Short- and Long-term Goals—Developing Strategies for Success—Checking Career Action Preparation—Preparing Requests for Approval—Auditing Career Transition Progress

TA = Transition Accomplished

Review of Completed Career Action Steps —Assessment of Well-being

Figure 16. Overview of Worklife Satisfaction Formula.

1. Information Base

A comprehensive record of education, non-work, and paid and unpaid employment experiences is assembled, together with personal data relevant to lifestyle and obligations to others. Plans for the future, if already developed, are highlighted.

2. Abilities and Skill Preferences Analysis

Each person possesses a unique pattern of abilities, interests, and preferences. By means of thoroughly researched self-search stimulus questionnaires this information is derived and documented. Personal values are clarified. Skills are identified and the concept of skills being transferable between occupations and career paths is introduced. Structured exercises are used to help the process of skills analysis. (If you did the Biographical Review Exercise on page 77 you will have developed your ability to recognize what skills you have and those you prefer using.)

3. Work Environment Analysis

Compatibility with different types of employment/occupational environments is examined. Together with the preceding analysis, data are assembled that will indicate where the highest performance and most satisfaction will be found in future jobs.

4. Problem Identification

Our analysis should clarify what really are the worklife problems we are seeking to resolve. There may be several and so a procedure needs to be followed for putting them in order of highest need and degree of urgency for resolution.

5. Resources and Constraints Analysis

An appraisal of the boundaries of restraint within which we can decide on career action steps needs to be determined—our family situation, financial obligations, education level attained, together with an assessment of our degree of self-confidence and personal skills for managing a career transition. We need to also appraise our resources—monetary, support from others, our attitude and level of motivation for change, etc.—aspects of career decision making in which many fall into the trap of underestimating what they are capable of.

You are ready to leave the Self-Assessment Stage when:

- You can state what the real problem is . . . in writing

- You have a list of your transferable skills, needs, values, interests, and achievements to date

- You have a list of employment likes and dislikes . . . and your reasons for them

- You can list the expectations people important to you have of you

- You have a list of your personal constraints and of your resources

- You have a list of things which you now know bring you satisfaction, personal growth, and a greater liking of self

---

You begin recording in a journal your thoughts fears, frustrations, expectations, progress.

• *INTERPRETING DATA*

In this phase, the asembled data about self needs to be converted into career themes, i.e., indicators of the most critical factors about self to be incorporated when determining the exact nature of a career action step and in making an appropriate plan for it. Making data coherent is a challenging task and sometimes it is useful to consider the opinions of others you allow to review your assembled data. To utilize this data effectively, it is necessary to undertake a thorough analysis of what work and life management needs you wish to satisfy. A vision of the desired worklife situation which will meet them should be drafted. This latter procedure is essential for the next phase, opportunity awareness, to be carried out thoroughly.

The database of your experience has been assembled and thoroughly examined; interpretation has led to the formulation of specific career action steps, and personal confidence has risen through this increased self-awareness.

You are ready to leave the Interpreting Data Stage when:

• You have a summary of your preferred skills

• You have a summary of your essential needs, preferred interests, and identification of your real values

• You have consulted your mentor and/or counsellor and/or significant other

• You have a developing list of jobs or occupations or possible career action steps which could provide opportunities for improved worklife satisfaction

• You have worked out how to begin and see through your career transition journey

Your journal includes entries which point to a theme or themes which reflect your uniqueness as a human being and reveal your personal identity.

• *OPPORTUNITY AWARENESS (Identifying the options)*

Opportunity awareness involves incorporating the new and confirmatory knowledge you have gained about self and exploring what job and career path options can be matched to your needs defined in the self-assessment stage.

At this stage, one of the career transition hazards occurs. Fired by enthusiasm, eager to put into action this self-learning, you are likely to feel propelled towards implementation. The danger is that the database from which to formulate the action you should take is not yet complete. The career action plans being formulated are draft action plans only. They need to be verified. **Printed information** needs to be obtained from career information resources, employers, professional associations, libraries, and continuing education institutions. In fact, any literature is relevant if it is about the nature and environment of the proposed career action steps. But the true nature of occupations, work environments, courses of study can only be obtained in sufficient depth and volume by identifying, meeting, and **questioning** people who possess this information.

1. Organizational Research

This is where ways to assess and use all career-related facilities where you live and, if employed, within your organization are studied. The focus is on practical solutions to personal career needs that will be compatible with the needs and aims of the labor market situation. The intent is to expand your awareness of alternative options for growth and learn how to test possibilities against environmenental realities. Here the concept is introduced that moving upwards by seeking promotion is not the only way to go. The focus is first on deciding whether to enrich your current job situation and plan future career moves or to seek a position in a different occupation or with a different employer.

2. Networking (Research interviews)

The usually neglected, but most effective, career management strategy is explored and methods researched. How to go about obtaining answers to questions is studied, rehearsed, and put into action. This sharpens the self-concept, focuses expectations, and recruits others as respected allies and information resources.

3. Reality Testing

When a career action step is evolved and research interviews completed, you confront the choice of what career action step to take next. You can either proceed to seek a job, where relevant, or implement the action where you work. Alternatively, you can build into your career transition a further check to see whether this direction is really the one which is right for you to take. This involves reality testing; in other words, seeking out actual opportunities to experience the proposed direction. Reality testing will be discussed in more depth later.

You are ready to leave the Opportunity Awareness Stage when:

- You have explored one or more jobs and gathered relevant, realistic information

- You have a list of action steps for the job(s) or career action you are developing to improve your worklife satisfaction

- You have a list of "discarded" options, together with the reasons for your decision to discard them

- You have tested the reality of your preferred job or draft career action steps with either a mentor, counsellor, significant other, or an appropriate expert

- You have collected appropriate information and planned what you will do with it

- You have prepared a draft version of your career accomplishment strategy and short-term plan with dates for achievement of the different steps towards fulfillment

---

Your journal reflects a number of creative thoughts and realistic ideas about career and life management action steps.

• *DECISION LEARNING (How to prepare for and make relevant decisions)*

1. Formulation of Goals/Career Goal Statement

Here all the data from the self-assessment, interpreting data and opportunity awareness stages are drawn together and assessed. A number of alternatives are likely to emerge as appropriate career action steps. Each needs to be evaluated and a selection made of the career action step to be implemented first. You arrive at and record a clear and concise current job career action and future career path objective, plus the schedule for its attainment. Personal preparation programs for short- and long-term objectives form an important part of this process.

2. Consultation

Rarely does worklife review and career pathing concern only you. Emphasis is here placed on the involvement of significant people in your life and their desires/expectations are incorporated. Where there are conflicts, indications of how and when these can be resolved need to be incorporated.

3. Mentoring

This involves learning how to select and recruit a mentor (sometimes termed a coach). A mentor can observe and identify the critical areas of a career action plan that requires refinement, and can provide feedback in a way that brings about an improvement in the overall result.

We all need a mentor/coach to bring out our best performance—a person with whom we can share our hopes and disappointments in an unfettered way, and who can review the proposed next step in our career transition. Feedback from a mentor can help us make decisions with more confidence.

You are ready to leave the Decision Learning Stage when:

- You have identified what kind of person you really are and determined what you want to do with the next two years of your life

- You have achieved this by discovering where you are today, how you got here, and where you now want to go

- You have considered a number of options for a decision, determined the decision criteria and the weighting appropriate to each criterion

- You make decisions based on what you have learned

- You carry out a decision using appropriate assertive behavior (as practice for larger decisions)

- You have a thoughtfully written version of your career strategy and have discussed the strategy and its rationale with your counsellor or mentor and/or significant other

Your journal records a growing confidence in your ability to reach and implement decisions which satisfy you, contribute to your career development and life management strategy, and indicate progress in enhancing the management of the way you live.

• *TRANSITION TRAINING (Preparing and implementing the desired and validated change)*

Transition training demands many skills and requires considerable information relevant to the career action decided upon. For example:

1. Strategy Selection

Career action strategies are studied and options recorded and analyzed. Once the objective is clear, materials are prepared and techniques well rehearsed, the career action is carefully planned, with steps to control, monitor, and ensure successful outcomes. An audit is carried out of what skills need to be improved in order to implement the career action step.

2. Communications

It is useful to undertake specific study on how to improve abilities, confidence, and style in communicating with other people, whether by memo, telephone, face-to-face or through job-seeking applications; once learned, these skills need to be tested.

3. Résumé Design

Résumé design may need to be studied. Several drafts may be produced before a final version is selected for use in internal applications such as promotion or transfer, or in searching for an alternative employer.

4. Interview Skills

The structure of the interview process, such as screening, selection, and panel, is examined from both the interviewer's and applicant's (your) perspectives. Also career review and performance appraisal discussions with one's current manager may need to be planned and rehearsed. Study of behavioral styles, conversational techniques, the effect the clothes and colors you wear have on others, using your voice to influence others, and body language feature in this.

5. Self-Management Skills

Stress management, testing out the reality of the proposed career action, conflict resolution and negotiating skills are likely to be needed among self-help approaches you may have to study and practice.

6. Rehearsal

(a) **The presentation of personal plans to a mentor, counsellor or career development trainer.** You prepare and make a presentation of your career action plans to another person. In the process, each step of the planned campaign is reviewed and audited in order to reduce anxiety and increase confidence. This provides an opportunity to diagnose where more learning is needed, to practice giving and receiving help from peers, and to identify concerns which need to be addressed further.

(b) **Personal planning without help.** When working alone on a career transition, essentially the same procedure is necessary in order to reduce the risks of the impending career transition to those risks which are worth taking. Use of self-directed publications[1] purchased from publishers or obtained from a counsellor engaged in career assistance, helps you complete the transition training on your own.

You are ready to leave the Transition Training Stage when:

• You can describe and explain the career and life management steps of your planned transition in terms of:

   * disengagement from past or current dissatisfiers

   * disentanglement from the influences of others not relevant to your real needs

   * expectations of positive growth as a result of your transition

• You can confidently explain these steps and your plans for managing each step to your mentor, counsellor, trainer or significant other,

• You have researched, evaluated, and decided how you will get where you want to be

• You have identified what skills need to be improved, the source from which this help can be obtained, and have started study to improve skills, and have rehearsed and practiced them

> Your journal indicates increasing confidence and readiness to apply your new skills and personal career and life management resolutions.

• *TRANSITION ACCOMPLISHED*

After a short time in the new career situation an audit should be carried out to review your degree of well-being. Reference may need to be made back to the self-assessment phase to monitor that intended improvements have, in fact, been achieved.

It is also a time to indulge comfortably in self-satisfaction. The career journey at this particular stage of life has been completed. This has been achieved by discovering a more accurate view of self and resolving to act to bring worklife more in line with who you truly are.

> Your Transition is complete when:
>
> • Your experiences and your career strategy become one
>
> • You become aware that others notice—and benefit from— your improved inner well-being
>
> Your journal reflects your pride in your accomplishments in self-exploration and in your career transition journey, your progress, and growing self-satisfaction. As well, it should outline any perceived obstacles to being able to protect your achievement and should include some humorous, even poignant, reflections on your experiences during this thorough review!

Bibliography and Useful Further Reading

Bolles, Richard Nelson, *How to Find Your Mission in Life,* Ten Speed Press, Berkeley, California, 1991.

Bolles, Richard Nelson. *What Color Is Your Parachute?,* Ten Speed Press, Berkeley, California, 1993 edition.

Calvert, Roy; Durkin, Brian; Grandi, Eugenio; and Martin, Kevin. *First Find Your Hilltop: Take control of your career by finding out who you are, where you want to be and how to get there,* Hutchinson Business Books, Sydney, 1990.

Charland, W. *Career Shifting: Starting Over in a Changing Economy,* Bob Adams Inc., Holbrook, Massachusetts, 1993.

Garafalo, Gene. *Hit the Ground Running,* Prentice Hall, New Jersey, 1993.

Guterman, Mark. *Common Sense for Uncommon Times: The Power of Balance in Work, Family and Personal Life,* Consulting Psychological Press, Palo Alto, California, 1994.

Hollander, Dr. Dory. *The Doom Loop System: A step-by-step guide to career mastery,* Viking Penguin, New York, 1991.

Jaffe, Dr. Betsy. *Altered Ambitions, What's Next in Your Life?* Donald I. Fine, Inc., New York, 2nd Edition, 1991.

Levinson, H. (editor). *Designing and Managing Your Career,* Harvard Business School Press, Boston, 1989.

Radin, Bill. *Take this Job & Leave It: How to get out of a job you hate and into a job you love,* Career Press Inc., Hawthorne, New Jersey, 1992.

Stevens, Paul. *How to Network and Select a Mentor,* The Centre for Worklife Counselling, Sydney, 2nd Edition, 1992.

Strasser, Dr. Stephen and Sena, Dr, John. *Transitions: Successful strategies from mid-career to retirement,* Career Press Inc., Hawthorne, New Jersey, 1992.

PART **3**

Overcoming Career Transition Pitfalls

- Emotion management
- Managing self-development
- Research interviews
- Reality testing
- Career transition loneliness
- Underestimating job-seeking complexity
- Bibliography and useful further reading

. . . .

When you believe that *Life*-is-career, you begin to place greater trust in *Life*. As you do, you find yourself *attracting* good fortune.

Anna Miller-Tiedeman
How NOT to Make it . . . And Succeed
(Lifecareer Foundation, 1989)

It is amazing how often people do get their dreams, whether in stages or directly. The more you don't *cut* the dream down, because of what you *think* you know about *the real world,* the more likely you are to find what you are looking for.

Richard Nelson Bolles
What Color is Your Parachute?
(Ten Speed Press, 1993 ed.)

. . . .

Emotion Management

I am filling you in on the vicissitudes of this career change business. I've run the full gamut through elation to depression and no doubt at each stage my equilibrium would have been somewhat different.

There can be many impediments to managing the complexity of career transition activities. You may have incomplete information about yourself or your options, or may be resisting the conclusion you have reached from the information you have gathered about yourself and your options. You may be experiencing difficulty in making the choice. And, understandably, apprehension about the possibility of failure as a result of implementing the proposed career action.

Planning and implementing a career transition always involves the expectation of some loss as well as gain, and letting go can be difficult. It helps to remind ourselves of what we have and what we are moving towards, rather than dwelling on what will be missing. A client wrote to me from another state some time after her career transition from teaching was completed and expressed this feeling in this way: "I have and still will have to accept the pain, the sense of loss and sadness that goes with letting go of the familiar and that with which I have identified myself for so long."

Keeping physically active is important to this mood control. Brisk walks, projects around the home and a clear-out of outdated clothes help to keep things in perspective and avoid wavering from your intent to alter the current unsatisfactory worklife situation. Mental clarity is important for achieving a new worklife situation. The thoroughness of your preparation can reduce the likelihood of pitfalls. Pause in your reading and complete Figure 17 to check your readiness.

Once in the new career situation you must continue to be in control. Figure 18 gives 16 tips that can help you manage your career situation.

Check Your Career Action-step Preparation

	Yes	No
• I am clear on the essential requirements in my next career move.	☐	☐
• I have recorded an unambiguous goal and a schedule for achieving each stage towards it.	☐	☐
• I have reexamined my values, which underpin my job satisfaction needs.	☐	☐
• I have a good understanding of my potential and where it can be realized.	☐	☐
• I have developed an action plan for enhancing the quality of my non-work activities.	☐	☐
• I know what to do to improve the blending of my career with my role as a family member, citizen, and learner	☐	☐
• I have a good grasp of self-help measures to improve my personal career management.	☐	☐
• I have sorted out my key strengths, interests, and motivations in relation to my worklife.	☐	☐
• I have conducted a thorough exploration of the employment market so that realistic alternatives can be pursued if necessary.	☐	☐

Figure 17. Check Your Career Action-step Preparation.

16 Tips for Protecting Your New Career Situation Effectively

1. Perform efficiently those job tasks which will help your boss the most.

2. Find out what your boss regards as good performance in your job. It may differ from your current opinion.

3. Master your job as quickly as possible and pass your knowledge to another person. In this way, lack of a suitable replacement will not stop your promotional chances.

4. Learn to like yourself as a precious unique human being. There is no need for you to wait in the wings. You need to move yourself into the spotlight so others can see, respect, and take notice of you.

5. Step outside the confines of your job description; make sure your actions are regarded as constructive initiative—not just attention seeking.

6. Don't agree to a promotion if it contains activities you don't like. We perform better when doing things we enjoy.

7. Expand opportunities for those in power to learn more about you by achieving success in outside work activities such as in community service organizations and/or personal development studies.

8. Identify a well-regarded person in a senior position within your employment environment from whom to seek career advancement advice, and return the favor with loyalty and respect.

9. Suggest thoroughly prepared recommendations—not criticisms—for problems within your employment environment.

continued

Figure 18. 16 Tips for Protecting Your New Career Situation Effectively.

10. Develop your skills at interpersonal relationships; accept the fact that office politics exist; reexamine your personal values regularly so that when faced with ethical dilemmas at work you will know what to do without procrastination.

11. Recognize that ability alone will not advance your career—persistence, hard work, and being seen as personally ambitious—but being an effective teamworker will.

12. Smile a lot. Others notice and favor people with happy but conscientious dispositions. Despondent people are often regarded as too risky to move to new positions.

13. Ensure you have a good variety of interests outside your worklife career to prevent the stress of your efforts bringing you harm.

14. Practice self-nomination. Don't wait to be offered promotion or transfer. Let it be known what different position you want and present a case for why you merit it.

15. Plan for more than one career path. Ensure you develop skills/knowledge for different types of positions. First, because you will then be better placed to take advantage of opportunities. Second, as a protection against falling behind in your knowledge and skills development.

16. Change employers only after deep thought and thorough research. Accept a new position not just for more pay but primarily for opportunities for new knowledge in your field.

Figure 18 (continued).

Managing Self-development

In choosing areas of new learning that we wish to pursue for our self-development, we should seek to enhance our experience. As has been emphasized, it is better to base our learning pursuits on those experiences we enjoy doing and learning about. This is likely to strengthen our motivation for further self-development and sustain us through any of the difficulties we experience in the course of our self-development. One danger in the selection of new learning is to give insufficient consideration to the ways we have learned best in the past.

People learn in different ways. Our learning behaviors differ. Some prefer learning in an environment where other people are pursuing the same quest, others prefer self-paced, self-managed learning. We may prefer the physical presence of a teacher or using open-learning education media such as workbooks, texts, software. We may prefer to study the theories upon which the content is based, or to carry out tasks experientially.

The objective in our choice of self-development activities is to facilitate some change in ourselves and often in others with whom we interact. It may be an increase in knowledge, learning a new skill or enhancing effectiveness in a skill we have already developed to some level. The decision about what the activity will be must be linked to the learning objective. Why do we want to pursue this? What will be the gain? Who will benefit from the achievement? Our career planning and life management goals have a direct bearing on how we arrive at the answers to these questions. Linked self-development makes the pursuit both valid and worthwhile. Once a decision is made, then we should set out to identify the facilities available for undertaking the activity.

We may choose to study a subject and seek experience in a particular activity associated with our work environment. Or we may choose to acquire knowledge for its sake alone. Whether we choose a study of financial balance sheets, Egyptology, Renaissance poetry, or presentation skills, we need to understand why we have selected the self-development activity. A more enriching learning experience will result. A more beneficial contribution to the way we live will result.

Protecting yourself during a career action step to avoid a burnout situation requires skill in political behavior, which figures in all employment environments. Check your skills with the questionnaire in Figure 19, "Understanding Office Politics."

Understanding Office Politics

Action: Consider each of these statements. Decide which are True, and which are False. Reflect on your worklife experiences to help you form your opinion. Discuss your opinions with your mentor, career counsellor, or a trusted friend or work colleague.

	True	False
• Power and politics are nasty business. Only the un-talented, incompetent, and perverse ignore them.	☐	☐
• Only people in staff management are in a position to gain and keep power.	☐	☐
• On balance, hard work is less important to success than are power and politics.	☐	☐
• Power within organizations is not unfair.	☐	☐
• Company functions such as staff parties and dinners are important political and power occasions.	☐	☐
• The closer you get to colleagues, the more involved you become in their goals and needs, the more likely you are to get cooperation from them when you need it.	☐	☐
• Your professional skills and knowledge are an important political and power tool.	☐	☐
• On the job nearly everyone is a role player.	☐	☐
• Advancement does not always have a direct relationship to productivity and creativity.	☐	☐
• In advancing your career you are more at risk from envious peers than from bosses.	☐	☐

Figure 19. Understanding Office Politics.

	True	False
• A good form of career self-defense is to maintain a written record of your work accomplishments.	☐	☐

Action: If you found your discussions useful, continue with the statements below.

	True	False
• Proposing the benefits to your listener and the organization is the best way to secure a career advancement.	☐	☐
• People are not too unpredictable to learn how to get along with them.	☐	☐
• Conflict is a daily reality for everyone.	☐	☐
• When using the confrontation strategy in resolving conflict, the negotiation approach allows both people to win whereas use of the power strategy results in one losing.	☐	☐
• Office politics determines who will get ahead.	☐	☐
• It is generally unwise to be open and trusting in relationships at work.	☐	☐
• Fewer people are terminated from their employment because of interpersonal office politics than because of poor work performance.	☐	☐
• The game of office politics is pretty much the same no matter where you work.	☐	☐
• One should go after job tasks that provide an opportunity to make you more positively visible within the organization.	☐	☐
• It is possible to learn how to say "No" firmly to supervisors and/or colleagues and not create resentment.	☐	☐
• Assessing the implications of changes in organizational structure is important.	☐	☐

Figure 19 (continued).

Research Interviews

I have learned something about the tourist industry that
makes me feel that it doesn't match up with me . . . it's the
glued-on nails and nailed-on hair styles.

Most people in career transition balk at the prospect of carrying out research interviews because they do not have sufficient faith that people will be prepared to share information, particularly when no payment is involved. They can also hesitate because they doubt that they have the interpersonal skills to elicit this information from strangers. There is no easy way to overcome these apprehensions. Each person needs to experiment before learning that this data is available from other people and will be readily shared.

You will need to read about, observe, and develop questions to ask people who can provide information about your proposed career action step. Your quest for information will be related to the nature of your particular career direction as it has evolved from your analysis and consultations with others. It is, however, likely to include the following:

- What are the special training/credentials associated with it?

- What are the survival skills needed to protect the career action step when taken?

- What are the skills most frequently required in performing the tasks associated with it?

- What are the lifestyle implications associated with the demands of this career action step?

- What employment environment features does it possess?

- What political skills and behaviors are significant for success in it?

- What is the most expeditious route to achieving entry or a transition to it?

When people set out on this quest for "real" information they have several advantages. The most important is that they are non-threatening. They are not approaching a person who has the information they need in search of a decision, a job offer, for money, or anything other than their time. Second, most people respect others who are taking care about their career planning, and to declare this early to the prospective information giver is most important. We do like talking about what we do. People like to give advice. They're flattered to be asked for their opinion. Do not deprive research interview prospects of the pleasure of talking about themselves! From the data obtained through research interviews you will be in a better position to evaluate your proposed career action steps in relation to their own needs and determinations for enhancing your career.

Reality Testing

I have found out that I would not prosper in a large organization with a rigid and immutable bureaucratic structure, if only because I would tread on too many powerful toes in the first twenty minutes of employment.

The commitment to the career action choice is a strategic milestone in career transitions. It is wise, when reaching this stage, to pause and enjoy the experience for a few days. This allows you to strengthen your resolve in the implementations stage. It will also allow time to practice providing reasons to others with whom you may share your resolution. For some, lingering doubts may need some period for reality testing. One form of reality testing is to seek temporary employment in a work situation closely resembling the one targeted by the career action. This may be achieved by taking extended leave from your current occupation and seeking casual or temporary employment in the targeted alternative. Sometimes opportunities can be found to experience the alternative through evening or weekend work, enabling you to remain in your current job until the experience has been evaluated.

In my experience with clients in career transitions, I have found too few people are prepared to invest time and effort in the reality testing phase. Many feel that the time, thoroughness, and emotional expenditure they have contributed to arriving at the implementation stage of the career transition journey are sufficient. They want to get on with their worklife in the newly chosen career action without further delay. The lack of reality testing does not necessarily jeopardize a satisfactory career transition outcome. It is just another step which further reduces the risks to those which are worth taking.

A high proportion of people who are in temporary employment are in fact searching for or evaluating *permanent* full-time employment. People who undertake temporary assignments not only acquire useful data about a proposed career path and the nature of employment environments but also quickly become familiar with the *hidden job market*. As a temporary, it is likely that a person will learn of the impending or actual vacancies which are not being or will not be advertised through recruitment advertisement or recruitment agencies. Real-world experiences gained while temping are useful for evaluating whether they match up with expectations and privately documented goals for career action.

Career Transition Loneliness

> *Being in my thirties, a single woman on welfare, and a stranger to my own country isn't a good basis for restarting a career.*

When working hard to progress a career, people often feel the need to talk to someone about their feelings and behavior.

While busy solving a series of worklife problems or carrying out the responsibilities of a job, it is difficult for us to observe ourselves and evaluate objectively our degree of readiness. What we consider to be appropriate behavior for our career action may not be compatible with the views or expectations of the employer or others important to us.

. . . .

> *My significant other can't understand me not getting satisfaction from work or not knowing what would give me career satisfaction.*

. . . .

A caution needs to be conveyed about the manner in which we communicate with friends, acquaintances, our manager at work, family members, and a partner such as a significant other. When we discuss personal data we may present ourselves to these people in a way that we have come to know they expect. Consequently, we may distort information about ourselves for the sake of the relationship, and the roles we play within it. Once alert to this danger, the degree of risk can be reduced. One procedure is to share some of the recordings made during the process of career analysis and personal data assembly, but retain your tentative conclusions. Then you can compare your private notes with the feedback you receive from the other person and note any differences. You may want to think about those differences and decide on communicating about them with the other person.

Underestimating Job-seeking Complexity

I believe most people who sit down with Sunday's newspaper want-ads put more thought and planning into their weekend game of golf or tennis than into the next step of their career. I have seen how well their golf and tennis goes, so what hope does their career have?

If you have experienced three or more job searches during your career, the complexity of the process will be of no surprise to you: the problem of how to design your résumé; the failure of employers' representatives to return your calls; the fluctuating emotions such as anxiety and stress, often experienced during selection interviews and when awaiting the verdict on your job applications. Many job seekers maintain for too long the fantasy that the right employer will discover them, make an employment offer, and hence these tribulations will be avoided. No personal effort to find a job is required. No effort made preparing and mailing 20 or more job applications a week. No experiencing the loneliness of the job search. The reality is, of course, very different.

The reality of job seeking also demands an understanding about what counts in securing reemployment. Getting a job offer is different from carrying out a particular job well. They are different situations and consequently demand different skills.

The skills required in job searching involve how the various job-seeking strategies are applied, how to present oneself at an interview and the character-testing attribute of persistence. Realistic expectations, the maintenance of enthusiasm, and a confident projection of self to others are essential. The inner person may feel depressed, handle rejections badly, and have moments of self-doubt, but these external characteristics need to be maintained. Concurrently, new skills relating to job seeking usually need to be learned and developed. Résumé writing, cover letter writing, conversational methods, appropriate assertiveness, and negotiation skills are critical to a successful outcome when job seeking is essential to implementing the career action step decision.

If job searching for an alternative employer is part of your career action resolution, then there is a need to pause and study the art of job seeking, and refine and rehearse the relevant skills before proceeding. Use Figure 20, "Check Your Job Hunt Preparation," as a checklist for those skills.

Check Your Job Hunt Preparation

	Yes	No
• I have identified my assets in terms of skills, abilities, and past achievements.	☐	☐
• I have identified my preferences for using my skills.	☐	☐
• I have thought about and defined the type of work and lifestyle I want.	☐	☐
• I have at least mentally summarized my personal experience in terms of work, education, and vocational activities.	☐	☐
• I have identified personality characteristics that should be considered in selecting my next boss.	☐	☐
• I know my feelings about the work environment setting I would like.	☐	☐
• I have researched at least three career path possibilities.	☐	☐

Figure 20. Check Your Job Hunt Preparation.

	Yes	No
• I have identified employers or people relevant to my career path choice.	☐	☐
• I have talked to two or more people in the field I am targeting.	☐	☐
• I have identified the relevant job titles I am considering.	☐	☐
• I have identified my needs for additional skill building which I should fulfill in my next job.	☐	☐
• I have obtained references from my past employer.	☐	☐
• I have prepared a good résumé and practiced writing cover letters.	☐	☐
• I know the kinds of questions to expect and ways to answer them.	☐	☐
• I have rehearsed the interview process with a reliable tutor.	☐	☐
• I have identified some employers I want to contact for interviews.	☐	☐
• I have, at least minimally, researched these employers.	☐	☐
• I have an understanding of the different approaches used to obtain interviews.	☐	☐
• I know what I want and how to go after it.	☐	☐
• I have reasonable alternatives in mind if initially unable to get my first choice.	☐	☐
• I have planned what clothes I will wear to interviews.	☐	☐

Figure 20 (continued).

Bibliography and Useful Further Reading

Brim, Gilbert. *Ambition: How We Manage Success and Failure Throughout Our Lives,* Basic Books (division of HarperCollins Publishers), New York, 1992.

Davidson, Frederick. *Handbook of Executive Survival,* The Business Library, Information Australia, Melbourne, 1991.

Figler, Howard. *The Complete Job Search Handbook: All the skills you need to get any job and have a good time doing it,* Henry Holt and Company, New York, 2nd edition, 1988.

Medley, H. Anthony. *Sweaty Palms: The Neglected Art of Being Interviewed,* Ten Speed Press, Berkeley, California, 2nd edition, 1992.

Scott, Gini. *The Empowered Mind: How to Harness the Creative Force Within You,* Prentice Hall, New Jersey,, 1994.

Solomon, Muriel. *Getting Praised, Raised and Recognized,* Prentice Hall, New Jersey, 1993.

Stevens, Paul. *Win That Job!* The Centre for Worklife Counselling, Sydney, 6th edition, 1991.

Stevens, Paul. *Handling Office Politics,* The Centre for Worklife Counselling, Sydney, 2nd edition, 1990.

Wesley, K. and Silverman, S. *Working Scared: Achieving Success in Trying Times,* Jossey-Bass Publishers, San Francisco, 1993.

THE PLEASURE
OF
HELPING

Worklife counselling involves its own special difficulties and challenges: the considerable amount of information acquired, analyzed, and used; the limitations of each client's situation; and fluctuating morale, occasional setbacks, and sometimes slow progress. Nevertheless, worklife counsellors help make dreams happen. We restore flagging spirits and are privileged to observe the emerging resilience of people who are often grappling with emotional pain. Concurrently, we strive to improve the manner of the support we apply; to listen to ourselves as we work and note where successful career transition support approaches occur and where enhancements to our counselling and support style and methods can be made.

We see overwhelming evidence that when you find your **passion**, your job is no longer work. Once you find it, you will, in effect, not **work** another day again!

For me, the pleasure of helping comes from doing what I want to do and like. Equally, it comes from observing the progress a person makes through the career transition process. I know many other career support counsellors feel the same way. I have chosen to end this book by including more quotations from my clients in the concluding phase of their transition journeys. These convey the pleasure of helping, as well as the joy, and the sense of renewed passion they have developed for work. My admiration for them remains undiminished.

· · · · · · · · · ·

Changing my career has presented a valuable growth experience. I feel I now have power to do anything I really want to do. I am in control again.

The personal worth of taking the career actions was evident almost immediately. My life is easier and without so many conflicts as before because I am more content, happier, and satisfied.

I have decided to learn more about psychology and maybe about literature. I want to learn about counselling and develop my skills in writing. I'd like to improve my oral communication skills, maybe even learn to speak effectively in public in order to teach. I will develop my skills in lateral thinking, in creative problem solving, and in drama, perhaps with a view to the use of drama in psychology and teaching. I want to learn about debating and arguing, and hypnosis. I do not wish for more knowledge about any aspect of my present job and career. I've learned where my efforts should best be placed for me!

The cost of this change, or realization of the truth, is without doubt the most shattering experience I have ever encountered. My experience has led to most satisfying results but, boy! I will never forget these events.

I don't say I enjoyed the traumas of the career transition experience which led me where I am but I'm happy they occurred—they let me face up to myself, my life, and made me decide what I wanted to be and do.

I have and still have to accept the pain, the sense of loss and sadness that goes with letting go of the familiar and that career with which I have identified myself for so long.

I feel you gave me the release to:
Go and Do Whatever I want to do
Gain a sense of self-worth, self-understanding
It is OK to be lost and searching
OK to be selfish

Thank you for helping this butterfly find her true colors!

. . . .

APPENDIX
· · · · · · · ·

PUBLICATIONS CONTAINING
SETS OF
STIMULUS QUESTIONNAIRES

Bloch, Dr. Deborah Permutter. *How to Make the Right Career Moves,* VGM Career Horizons, Lincolnwood, Illinois, 1990.

Bolles, Richard Nelson. *How to Create a Picture of Your Ideal Job or Next Career,* Ten Speed Press, Berkeley, California, 1991.

CEPEC Limited. *Life and Career: A self-development workbook,* CEPEC Limited, London, 1992.

Clawson, J. and Kotter, J. *Self-Assessment and Career Development,* Prentice-Hall, New York, 1985 edition.

Goodman, Jane and Hoppin, Judith M. *Opening Doors: A practical guide for job hunting,* Continuum Center, Oakland University, Rochester, NY, (2nd edition) 1990.

Guterman, Mark. *The Employees' Career Planning Workbook: A guide to managing your career in times of change,* G & G Associates, California, 1990.

Hirsch, Arlene S. *VGM's Career Checklists: 89 proven checklists to help you plan your career and get great jobs,* VGM Career Horizons, Lincolnwood, Illinois, 1991.

Moses, Dr. B.B. *Career Planning Workbook,* BBM Human Resource Consultants, Inc., Toronto, Canada, 1989.

Stevens, Paul. *Your Career Planner: Reducing the risks to those worth taking,* The Centre for Worklife Counselling, Sydney, 1991.

VGM CAREER BOOKS

CAREER DIRECTORIES
Careers Encyclopedia
Dictionary of Occupational
Titles
Occupational Outlook
Handbook

CAREERS FOR
Animal Lovers
Bookworms
Computer Buffs
Crafty People
Culture Lovers
Environmental Types
Film Buffs
Foreign Language Aficionados
Good Samaritans
Gourmets
History Buffs
Kids at Heart
Nature Lovers
Night Owls
Number Crunchers
Plant Lovers
Shutterbugs
Sports Nuts
Travel Buffs

CAREERS IN
Accounting; Advertising;
Business; Child Care;
Communications; Computers;
Education; Engineering;
the Environment; Finance;
Government; Health Care;
High Tech; Journalism; Law;
Marketing; Medicine;
Science; Social &
Rehabilitation Services

CAREER PLANNING
Admissions Guide to Selective
Business Schools
Beating Job Burnout
Beginning Entrepreneur
Career Planning &
Development for College
Students & Recent Graduates
Career Change

Careers Checklists
Cover Letters They Don't
Forget
Executive Job Search Strategies
Guide to Basic Cover Letter
Writing
Guide to Basic Resume Writing
Guide to Temporary
Employment
Job Interviews Made Easy
Joyce Lain Kennedy's Career
Book
Out of Uniform
Resumes Made Easy
Slam Dunk Resumes
Successful Interviewing for
College Seniors
Time for a Change

CAREER PORTRAITS
Animals   Nursing
Cars   Sports
Computers   Teaching
Music   Travel

GREAT JOBS FOR
Communications Majors
English Majors
Foreign Language Majors
History Majors
Psychology Majors

HOW TO
Approach an Advertising
Agency and Walk Away with
the Job You Want
Bounce Back Quickly After
Losing Your Job
Choose the Right Career
Find Your New Career Upon
Retirement
Get & Keep Your First Job
Get Hired Today
Get into the Right Business
School
Get into the Right Law School
Get People to Do Things Your
Way
Have a Winning Job Interview

Hit the Ground Running in
Your New Job
Improve Your Study Skills
Jump Start a Stalled Career
Land a Better Job
Launch Your Career in TV
News
Make the Right Career Moves
Market Your College Degree
Move from College into a
Secure Job
Negotiate the Raise You
Deserve
Prepare a Curriculum Vitae
Prepare for College
Run Your Own Home Business
Succeed in College
Succeed in High School
Write a Winning Resume
Write Successful Cover Letters
Write Term Papers & Reports
Write Your College Application
Essay

OPPORTUNITIES IN
This extensive series provides
detailed information on nearly
150 individual career fields.

RESUMES FOR
Advertising Careers
Banking and Financial Careers
Business Management Careers
College Students &
Recent Graduates
Communications Careers
Education Careers
Engineering Careers
Environmental Careers
50 + Job Hunters
Health and Medical Careers
High School Graduates
High Tech Careers
Law Careers
Midcareer Job Changes
Sales and Marketing Careers
Scientific and Technical Careers
Social Service Careers
The First-Time Job Hunter